Git Mastery: Version Control for Developers

A Step-by-Step Guide to Mastering Git for Collaborative Coding

MIGUEL FARMER

RAFAEL SANDERS

Table of Content

TABLE OF CONTENTS

INTRODUCTION

Mastering Git: A Comprehensive Guide for Collaborative Coding

In the world of modern software development, version control is indispensable. It empowers teams to collaborate effectively, ensures that every change is documented, and makes it possible to recover from mistakes without jeopardizing the stability of a project. **Git**, a distributed version control system (DVCS), has become the gold standard for managing source code. Whether you're working on a solo project or contributing to large-scale enterprise applications, Git's power and flexibility have made it the go-to tool for developers worldwide.

This book, *Mastering Git: A Comprehensive Guide for Collaborative Coding*, is designed to take you on a journey from basic concepts to advanced Git practices, providing you with the skills and knowledge you need to become a Git master. While Git can seem overwhelming at first, especially when dealing with complex workflows, this guide aims to break down those complexities in a way that is accessible and engaging, helping you navigate through Git's many features and use cases, all the way to mastering collaborative workflows with your team.

Whether you're a beginner trying to understand what version control is all about or an experienced developer looking to improve your workflows, this book will serve as a valuable resource at every stage of your Git journey.

Why Git? Why Now?

Git's rise to prominence is no accident. As software development has grown increasingly complex, Git has evolved to meet the demands of modern development practices. Unlike traditional centralized version control systems (CVCS), Git's **distributed architecture** allows every developer to have a full-fledged of the repository, enabling **offline work**, **fast branching**, and **powerful merging**. These features have made Git indispensable, especially in large, distributed teams that need to collaborate seamlessly.

The widespread adoption of Git can be attributed to its speed, efficiency, and flexibility, along with a vast ecosystem of tools like **GitHub**, **GitLab**, and **Bitbucket** that enhance its capabilities. From **collaborative open-source**

projects to **enterprise-level applications**, Git is the foundation that underpins modern development workflows.

What You'll Learn

This book is designed to guide you through Git, from basic concepts to advanced usage, all while emphasizing collaborative coding practices. Here's what you can expect to learn:

1. **Foundational Concepts**:
   - Learn what version control is, why it matters, and how Git works under the hood.
   - Understand how to use basic Git commands like `git init`, `git add`, `git commit`, and `git push`.
2. **Mastering Git Workflows**:
   - Understand essential workflows such as **Git Flow**, **GitHub Flow**, and **GitLab Flow**, and learn how to choose the right one for your team.
   - Gain hands-on experience with **branching and merging** to work on features in parallel, fix bugs, and integrate changes efficiently.
3. **Collaboration Best Practices**:

- o Learn how to collaborate effectively using **feature branches**, **pull requests**, and **code reviews**.

- o Understand how to manage **conflicts** and use tools like **Git rebase**, **git cherry-pick**, and **git stash** to resolve issues and keep your history clean.

4. **Advanced Git Features**:

- o Dive deeper into Git's more advanced features, such as **Git submodules**, **Git hooks**, **Git bisect**, and **Git LFS** (Large File Storage).

- o Discover how to use Git for **Infrastructure as Code (IaC)** and manage **automated deployment pipelines** in a DevOps environment.

5. **Real-World Scenarios**:

- o The book includes **real-world examples** and case studies that illustrate how Git is used in professional development environments. You'll also get insights into **migrating to Git** from other version control systems and integrating Git into existing workflows.

Who This Book is For

This book is intended for developers at various stages of their careers:

- **Beginners**: If you're new to version control, this book will guide you step-by-step through Git's essential commands, workflows, and best practices. You'll start by setting up your first Git repository, making commits, and learning how to collaborate with others.

- **Intermediate Developers**: If you already have some experience with Git but want to enhance your skills, this book will introduce you to **advanced Git features** like rebasing, resolving merge conflicts, using submodules, and applying Git in **DevOps** pipelines. You'll also learn how to **optimize your workflows** for team collaboration.

- **Advanced Developers**: If you're an experienced developer looking to sharpen your Git expertise, this book will provide deep insights into managing large-scale codebases, mastering Git's more intricate features, and adopting the latest Git tools and practices in collaborative and enterprise settings.

Why Git Mastery is Essential

Mastering Git is essential not just for developers, but for anyone involved in the software development lifecycle. Git's efficiency and power extend beyond basic code management—it's integral to **team collaboration, CI/CD pipelines, testing, deployment**, and even **infrastructure management**. Here are a few reasons why mastering Git is crucial:

1. **Collaboration**: Git makes it easy for developers to work on different parts of a project at the same time. By mastering Git workflows, you can ensure that collaboration with your team is smooth and conflict-free.

2. **Code Quality**: Git encourages smaller, incremental changes, making it easier to maintain high code quality. Commit messages, code reviews, and merge strategies all contribute to a well-maintained, easy-to-read codebase.

3. **Automation and DevOps**: Git plays a central role in **DevOps** pipelines, helping automate processes like testing, deployment, and infrastructure management. By understanding Git's integration with **CI/CD**

tools, you can ensure that your development cycle is efficient, reliable, and scalable.

4. **Long-Term Codebase Health**: A clean Git history makes it easier to manage and maintain codebases in the long term. This is crucial in large projects with many contributors, as it helps track the evolution of the code, identify bugs, and revert changes when necessary.

A Comprehensive Journey

This book is structured in a way that takes you from understanding the basics of Git to applying advanced techniques in real-world scenarios. It is divided into clear sections to guide you through your learning journey:

1. **Foundations**: Basic Git commands, version control principles, and common workflows.
2. **Collaboration**: Best practices for working in teams, resolving conflicts, and managing branches.
3. **Advanced Git**: In-depth coverage of advanced features like rebasing, submodules, Git hooks, and more.

4. **DevOps and Automation**: Integrating Git into **CI/CD pipelines** and managing infrastructure as code.

5. **Real-World Scenarios**: Practical examples and case studies of Git in action in large-scale projects.

Each chapter includes **hands-on exercises** and **real-world examples** to ensure that you gain practical experience with every concept covered.

The Road Ahead

Git is an essential tool that every developer should master. By diving deep into its features and workflows, you'll not only become proficient in version control but also improve your overall development practices. This book is designed to be both a **learning resource** and a **reference guide**—whether you're starting from scratch or looking to refine your existing knowledge.

As you complete this journey, you'll be equipped with the tools and strategies needed to collaborate effectively, manage complex projects, and contribute to software development in ways that streamline processes and deliver high-quality results. Whether you're working on **open-source projects**, in a **corporate team**, or leading your own development efforts, mastering Git will empower you to take control of your code and drive success in your projects.

So, let's begin the journey toward **becoming a Git master**!

CHAPTER 1

UNDERSTANDING VERSION CONTROL

Version control is a fundamental tool for developers, enabling them to track, manage, and collaborate on code changes. As projects grow in size and complexity, the ability to manage different versions of code becomes critical. This chapter will introduce **version control** and explore why it's essential in modern software development. We will also dive into the different types of version control systems: **local, centralized,** and **distributed**, providing a comprehensive understanding of how each works. Finally, we'll use a **real-world example** to show how version control helps developers in a team setting manage code changes effectively.

What is Version Control, and Why Is It Essential?

Version control is a system that helps software developers track changes to their codebase over time. It allows you to save different versions of your code, so you can easily revert to previous versions, track modifications, and collaborate with others without overwriting each other's work.

Here's why version control is essential:

1. **Tracking Changes**:
   - o As you work on a project, the code evolves. With version control, you can track what changes were made, who made them, and why they were made. This allows you to see the evolution of a project and troubleshoot issues more easily.

2. **Collaboration**:
   - o Developers often work in teams, and version control makes collaboration much more manageable. Without version control, coordinating work between team members can quickly become chaotic, with everyone working on the same file and potentially overwriting each other's changes. Version control resolves this by allowing each developer to work independently and then merge their changes smoothly.

3. **Reverting to Previous Versions**:

o Mistakes are inevitable, and when they happen, you want to be able to revert to a stable version of your code. Version control systems make it easy to roll back to a previous commit or version, minimizing downtime and disruptions.

4. **Branching and Experimentation**:

   o With version control, you can create **branches** to experiment with new features without affecting the main project. This allows you to develop new features in isolation, ensuring that the main branch remains stable.

5. **Audit Trail**:

   o Version control provides an audit trail of who made changes, when they made them, and what those changes were. This can be crucial for debugging, understanding the history of a project, and meeting compliance requirements.

Types of Version Control

There are three primary types of version control systems, each with its strengths and weaknesses. Let's break them down:

1. **Local Version Control**:

   o **Definition**: In **local version control**, each developer has their own of the entire project, including the code and all its changes. Changes are tracked only locally, so there is no central repository or shared history between developers.

   o **Advantages**: Simple to set up, no need for a server, and all changes are stored locally.

   o **Disadvantages**: Collaboration is very difficult since there's no easy way to share changes, track changes across team members, or merge different versions.

   Example: If you were working alone on a personal project, you might manually save different versions of your code in separate folders or files. However, this method doesn't scale well when working with others or on large projects.

2. **Centralized Version Control**:

   o **Definition**: In **centralized version control systems (CVCS)**, there is a central server that holds the project's version history. Developers check out files from the server, make changes, and then check those changes back in to the server. The server acts as the single point of truth for all changes.

- o **Examples**: Systems like **Subversion (SVN)** and **CVS** are examples of centralized version control systems.

- o **Advantages**: Provides a single central repository, which makes it easier to share and collaborate on code. It also ensures everyone works on the same version of the project.

- o **Disadvantages**: If the central server goes down, developers can't access or check in their changes. Also, the system can become slower as the project and team size grow.

Real-world example: A small team of developers working on a software product might use a centralized version control system like SVN. Each developer works on their local machine, but all changes are pushed to a central server, making it easier to track changes and collaborate. However, if the server goes down, no one can work.

3. **Distributed Version Control:**

   o **Definition: Distributed version control systems (DVCS)** are the most popular and modern approach to version control. In a DVCS, every developer has their own full of the repository, including its entire history. Developers can work on their local repositories and synchronize with other repositories when needed, such as by pushing and pulling changes to and from a central server.

   o **Examples: Git, Mercurial**, and **Bazaar** are examples of distributed version control systems.

   o **Advantages:** Every developer has a complete history of the project on their machine, making it fast and reliable. Developers can work offline, and synchronization can happen later. Git, for example, allows for powerful branching and merging capabilities.

   o **Disadvantages:** Because each developer has a full of the repository, the system can use more disk space. It also requires a more advanced setup compared to centralized systems.

22

Real-world example: Git is the most widely used DVCS today. Large open-source projects like **Linux** and **GitHub** use Git to enable collaboration. With Git, each contributor has a complete version history of the project on their machine, enabling them to work independently on their local repositories and merge their changes with the team later.

Real-World Example: Managing Code Changes in a Team of Developers

Let's look at a real-world example of how version control helps manage code changes in a development team. Suppose a team of developers is working on an e-commerce web application. The team includes a front-end developer, a back-end developer, and a tester.

1. **Branching for Feature Development**:
   o The team uses Git to manage their codebase. The front-end developer creates a branch called `feature/cart` to work on a new shopping cart feature, while the back-end developer creates a

23

`feature/payment` branch to implement the payment gateway.

- o Both developers work on their branches independently, making commits to their respective branches. The version control system keeps track of their changes.

2. **Merging Changes**:

- o Once the front-end and back-end developers finish their work, they merge their branches back into the main branch, often called `master` or `main`.

- o Git uses its merge mechanism to combine the changes. If there are conflicting changes (e.g., both developers modified the same file), Git will highlight the conflict and prompt the developers to resolve it.

3. **Collaboration with Remote Repositories**:

- o The team uses a central Git repository hosted on GitHub. Each developer clones the repository, allowing them to have a local of the project.

- o They frequently push their changes to the remote repository and pull the latest changes from their teammates. This ensures everyone is working on the latest version of the code, and the history of changes is stored centrally.

4. **Version History and Rollbacks**:

   o The version control system tracks every change, allowing the team to revert to previous versions if a feature breaks. For example, if the `feature/cart` branch introduces a bug, the team can check the Git history and roll back to a working version of the code.

Key Takeaways:

- **Version control** is essential for software development, enabling teams to collaborate, track changes, and maintain the integrity of codebases.

- **Local version control** is simple but lacks collaboration features.

- **Centralized version control** allows multiple developers to work on the same project, but has limitations regarding offline work and scalability.

- **Distributed version control**, such as Git, is the most modern and flexible system, allowing offline work and efficient collaboration across teams.
- In a **real-world project**, version control is crucial for managing branches, merging code, resolving conflicts, and tracking the history of changes.

By understanding the importance and functionality of version control systems, especially Git, you'll be well-equipped to handle versioning and collaboration in any software development project.

CHAPTER 2

GETTING STARTED WITH GIT

Git is one of the most powerful tools in a developer's toolkit, enabling version control and collaboration in software development. In this chapter, we'll introduce **Git**, explore why it's a popular choice over other version control systems, guide you through the installation process, and walk you through setting up your first Git repository. Finally, we'll touch on platforms like **GitHub** and **GitLab** that allow you to host and manage your repositories online.

What is Git? Why Choose Git Over Other Version Control Systems?

Git is a **distributed version control system** (DVCS) that allows developers to track changes in their code, collaborate with others, and manage multiple versions of a project efficiently. It was created by **Linus Torvalds** in 2005 to help manage the development of the **Linux kernel**, and since then, it has become the de facto standard for version control in software development.

Why Choose Git?

1. **Distributed Architecture**: Unlike centralized version control systems, where the central server stores all the code history, Git gives each developer a full of the repository, including its history. This allows for offline work, faster access to the repository, and more flexibility.

2. **Speed and Efficiency**: Git is known for its **speed**, especially when it comes to checking the status of files, switching branches, and committing changes. Git is optimized for performance and can handle large projects and repositories efficiently.

3. **Branching and Merging**: One of the most powerful features of Git is its **branching model**. You can easily create branches for different features, experiments, or fixes, and later merge them into the main branch. Git's merging capabilities are fast and reliable.

4. **Collaboration**: Git makes it easy to work with other developers, even on large teams. Each developer can work in isolation on their branch and then merge their changes into the main project seamlessly. It also integrates with popular platforms like **GitHub** and **GitLab** for collaborative workflows.

5. **Open Source and Free**: Git is an **open-source** tool, which means it's free to use, and anyone can contribute to its development. It's also widely supported by various platforms, editors, and tools.

Installing Git and Setting Up Your First Repository

To get started with Git, you'll need to install it on your machine. The installation process varies depending on your operating system, but Git supports all major platforms, including **Windows**, **macOS**, and **Linux**.

Installing Git on Windows:

1. Download the latest Git installer from the official website: Git Downloads.
2. Run the installer and follow the default installation steps.
3. Once installed, open the **Git Bash** terminal (which is provided by the Git installer) and type the following to verify the installation:

```
bash

git --version
```

You should see the version of Git you just installed, confirming that it's properly installed.

Installing Git on macOS:

1. If you have **Homebrew** installed, you can install Git by running:

    ```bash
    brew install git
    ```

    Alternatively, you can download the Git installer for macOS from the official Git website.

2. Verify the installation by running:

    ```bash
    git --version
    ```

Installing Git on Linux:

1. On **Ubuntu** or **Debian-based** systems, you can install Git by running:

    ```bash
    ```

```
sudo apt-get install git
```

For **Fedora** or **CentOS** systems, use:

```
bash
```

```
sudo dnf install git
```

2. Verify the installation by typing:

```
bash
```

```
git --version
```

Configuring Git:

Once Git is installed, it's time to set up your user information, which Git will use to track your commits.

1. Open your terminal and run the following commands, replacing the name and email with your own:

```
bash
```

```
git config --global user.name "Your Name"
git    config    --global    user.email
"your_email@example.com"
```

31

2. To verify the configuration, you can check your settings by running:

```bash

git config --global --list
```

Creating Your First Git Repository:

Now that Git is installed and configured, let's create your first repository.

1. Create a new directory for your project (or navigate to an existing one):

```bash

mkdir my_first_project
cd my_first_project
```

2. Initialize a Git repository in the directory:

```bash

git init
```

This will create a .git folder that Git uses to track changes in the directory.

3. Create your first file in the repository:

```bash
echo "Hello, Git!" > readme.txt
```

4. Add the file to the staging area:

```bash
git add readme.txt
```

5. Commit the file to the repository:

```bash
git commit -m "Initial commit: added readme.txt"
```

Your first commit has now been recorded in the version history.

Introduction to GitHub and GitLab for Hosting Repositories

Once you have your local repository set up, you may want to host it online for **collaboration**, **backup**, and **sharing** purposes. GitHub and GitLab are two of the most popular platforms for hosting Git repositories, offering features such as pull requests, issue tracking, and continuous integration.

GitHub:

- **GitHub** is the largest platform for hosting Git repositories. It provides a user-friendly interface for managing repositories, collaborating with others, and showcasing your projects.

- **Creating a GitHub Repository**:

  1. Go to GitHub and create an account if you don't have one.

  2. Click on the **New Repository** button to create a new project.

  3. Follow the prompts to name your repository, add a description, and choose privacy settings.

  4. After creating the repository, GitHub will show you the commands to link your local repository to the remote GitHub repository. Typically, the commands will look like:

  bash

```
git       remote       add       origin
https://github.com/your_username/yo
ur_repository.git
git push -u origin master
```

GitLab:

- **GitLab** is another Git hosting platform that provides features similar to GitHub, with an emphasis on DevOps and CI/CD (Continuous Integration and Continuous Deployment). It also offers private repositories for free, which can be a great option for private or internal projects.

- **Creating a GitLab Repository**:

  1. Go to GitLab and create an account.

  2. Create a new repository by clicking on **Create a project**.

  3. Follow the prompts to name your project and configure it.

  4. Similar to GitHub, GitLab will provide the URL and commands to link your local Git repository to the remote GitLab repository:

  bash

```
git        remote        add        origin
https://gitlab.com/your_username/yo
ur_repository.git
git push -u origin master
```

Real-World Example: Creating Your First Project with Git

Let's walk through an example to solidify your understanding of Git. Imagine you're working on a **personal website** project with a small team of developers.

Steps:

1. **Create a project directory** on your local machine and initialize Git:

   ```bash
   ```

   ```bash
   mkdir personal_website
   cd personal_website
   git init
   ```

2. **Create your project files**:

   ```bash
   ```

```
echo "<html><body>Welcome to my personal
website!</body></html>" > index.html
```

3. **Stage and commit the file**:

```bash
```

```
git add index.html
git commit -m "Initial commit: added
homepage"
```

4. **Create a GitHub or GitLab repository** and link it to your local repository:

```bash
```

```
git        remote        add        origin
https://github.com/your_username/personal
_website.git
git push -u origin master
```

5. **Collaborate with others**: Your team members can now clone the repository, make changes to different files, and push their updates. When changes are made, everyone can pull the latest code from the repository and push their own changes.

6. **Track progress with branches**: If you're working on a new feature (e.g., an **about page**), you can create a new branch and work on that feature without affecting the main project:

```bash
git checkout -b feature/about-page
```

Key Takeaways:

- **Git** is a powerful, distributed version control system that helps developers manage code changes, collaborate on projects, and maintain a history of their work.
- Installing Git is easy, and once set up, you can initialize a repository, make commits, and track changes locally.
- **GitHub** and **GitLab** are popular platforms for hosting Git repositories online, offering collaboration features like pull requests, issues, and CI/CD integration.
- By following real-world examples, you can quickly get started with Git, create your first project, and begin collaborating on larger, more complex software projects.

In the next chapter, we will dive deeper into the **Git workflow**, where you'll learn how to navigate your repositories, track changes, and explore powerful Git features that will help you manage even the most complex projects efficiently.

CHAPTER 3

GIT BASICS: YOUR FIRST COMMIT

Git is a powerful tool for version control, but understanding its fundamental operations is crucial to using it effectively. In this chapter, we'll explore the basic structure of a Git repository, how to stage and commit changes, and introduce the essential Git commands you'll use regularly. By the end of this chapter, you'll have created your first Git repository, added your first file, and made your first commit.

The Structure of a Git Repository

When you initialize a new Git repository, Git creates a hidden directory called `.git` inside your project folder. This directory is where all of Git's internal data and metadata are stored. It includes:

- **Commit history**: A record of all the changes made to your project over time.

- **Configuration files**: Information about the repository, such as remote repositories and user settings.
- **Staging area**: Where files are prepared for committing.

Git's structure can be broken down into three key areas:

1. **Working Directory**: The actual files you work on in your project. This is where your code lives.

2. **Staging Area (Index)**: A temporary area where changes are stored before they are committed. You add changes to the staging area using the `git add` command.

3. **Repository (Local Repository)**: The `.git` directory, where Git tracks all your commits, branches, and version history.

Think of the workflow like this:

- **Working Directory**: Where you make edits to files.
- **Staging Area**: The files you want to commit (i.e., the snapshot of changes you've made).
- **Repository**: The complete history of your project, where committed changes are stored permanently.

Staging and Committing Changes

When you make changes to your project files, Git allows you to decide which changes you want to keep track of and commit. This process happens in two steps: **staging** and **committing**.

1. **Staging Changes**:
   o After modifying a file in your working directory, you need to add it to the **staging area** before it can be committed. This tells Git which changes you want to include in your next commit.
   o The command to stage changes is:

   ```bash
   git add <filename>
   ```

   You can also stage all modified files with:

   ```bash
   git add .
   ```

2. **Committing Changes**:
   o A **commit** is like taking a snapshot of your staged changes and storing it in your repository's

42

history. Each commit has a unique ID (a long string of characters) and is accompanied by a commit message describing what was changed.

- The command to commit your staged changes is:

```bash

git commit -m "Your commit message"
```

The -m flag allows you to add a message directly from the command line.

Basic Git Commands

Let's now dive into the basic Git commands that form the foundation of your workflow.

1. **git init**: Initializes a new Git repository.
   - This command sets up the necessary files and directories for version control. It only needs to be run once when you start a new project.
   - Example:

```bash
```

```
git init
```

2. **git add**: Adds files to the staging area.

   o   After modifying files, use this command to tell Git which files you want to include in the next commit.

   o   Example (add a specific file):

   ```bash
   git add index.html
   ```

   o   Example (add all modified files):

   ```bash
   git add .
   ```

3. **git commit**: Saves changes to the local repository.

   o   After staging your changes, use this command to commit them to the Git repository.

   o   Example:

   ```bash
   git commit -m "Added homepage content"
   ```

4. **git status**: Shows the status of the working directory and staging area.

   o This command is useful for seeing which files are staged, which are modified, and which are untracked.

   o Example:

   ```bash
   ```

   ```
   git status
   ```

Real-World Example: Adding Your First File to a Git Repository and Committing Changes

Now, let's walk through a practical example of using these basic Git commands to create a new project, add your first file, stage changes, and make your first commit.

Step 1: Create a New Project Directory

First, create a new directory for your project:

```bash
```

```
mkdir my_first_git_project
cd my_first_git_project
```

Step 2: Initialize a Git Repository

Next, initialize Git in this project directory:

bash

```
git init
```

This command sets up a new Git repository and creates a hidden
.git folder in your project. You won't see this folder by default,
but it's where Git stores all of its tracking data.

Step 3: Create Your First File

Let's create a simple HTML file to work with:

bash

```
echo "<html><body><h1>Welcome to my first Git
project!</h1></body></html>" > index.html
```

Step 4: Check the Status of Your Repository

Use the `git status` command to see the state of your repository:

bash

```
git status
```

This will show that index.html is an **untracked file**, meaning Git doesn't yet know about it.

Step 5: Stage the File for Commit

Now, let's tell Git to start tracking the new file by adding it to the staging area:

bash

```
git add index.html
```

To check the status again and confirm that the file is staged:

bash

```
git status
```

You should see that index.html is now in the **staging area**, ready to be committed.

Step 6: Commit the Changes

Now that your file is staged, let's commit the changes to your local repository:

bash

```
git commit -m "Initial commit: added index.html"
```

The -m flag allows you to add a commit message, which is essential for keeping track of your project's history.

Step 7: Verify the Commit

You can check the commit history with:

```
bash
```

```
git log
```

This will show you a log of all commits made to the repository, including the commit you just made. The log will display the **commit ID**, the author's name, the date, and the commit message.

Key Takeaways:

- A **Git repository** is a folder where Git tracks changes to your files. Inside the repository, Git tracks changes in the **working directory**, **staging area**, and **repository**.
- The process of working with Git involves **staging** changes (with `git add`) and then **committing** them (with `git commit`), effectively creating snapshots of your project.
- The basic commands you'll use in every project include:

- o `git init` (to initialize a repository)

- o `git add` (to stage changes)

- o `git commit` (to commit changes)

- o `git status` (to see the status of your repository)

- In the real world, Git helps you track changes, collaborate with others, and maintain the integrity of your codebase.

Now that you've learned how to commit your first changes, you're ready to dive deeper into Git's powerful features, including branching and merging, which we'll cover in the next chapter. Git will soon become an indispensable tool in your development workflow!

CHAPTER 4

NAVIGATING YOUR GIT REPOSITORY

Once you've initialized a Git repository and started working with Git, it's important to understand how to navigate and interact with your repository effectively. This chapter will cover key commands like `git status` and `git log` that help you check your repository's state, explore the `.git` directory, and understand the fundamental components of a Git repository: the **working directory**, **staging area**, and **commit history**.

By the end of this chapter, you'll be able to track changes, understand your repository's state, and effectively view your project's history.

Using `git status` and `git log` to Check the Repository's State

Two of the most commonly used commands in Git are `git status` and `git log`. These commands help you keep track of changes and see the state of your repository at any given moment.

50

1. **git status**:

   o The git status command shows you the current state of your repository, including which files have been modified, which files are staged for the next commit, and which files are untracked (not yet added to Git).

   o Running git status will give you valuable information about your working directory and staging area.

Example:

bash

git status

You might see output like:

bash

On branch master
Your branch is up to date with 'origin/master'.

Changes not staged for commit:
  (use "git add <file>..." to update what will be committed)

```
    (use "git restore <file>..." to discard
changes in working directory)
    modified:    index.html

no changes added to commit (use "git add"
and/or "git commit -a")
```

- o **Working Directory Changes**: `index.html` is modified but hasn't been staged yet.

- o **Staging Area**: There are no changes staged for commit.

- o The command also gives helpful hints about how to add or restore files, making it easier to track your changes.

2. **git log**:

- o The `git log` command shows the commit history, including details like commit IDs, author information, dates, and commit messages.

- o This allows you to track the history of changes made to your project.

Example:

bash

```
git log
```

Example output:

```
bash
```

```
commit
a4b345df5f3d51f5a9b3d85d0fdd3f2e5fbbdbd4
Author: Your Name <your_email@example.com>
Date:   Mon Mar 28 13:43:20 2022 -0400

    Initial commit: added index.html

commit
567abc239f2a1344d7d9bb1a23fe2f3bd0b9b6fd
Author: Your Name <your_email@example.com>
Date:   Sun Mar 27 18:25:30 2022 -0400

    Created the repository and initialized
with README
```

o Each commit has a unique **commit hash** (a long string of characters like `a4b345df5f3d51f5a9b3d85d0fdd3f2e5fb bdbd4`), an **author**, a **timestamp**, and a **commit message**.

o You can use `git log` to view your entire commit history and see the progression of changes over time.

Exploring the `.git` Directory

The **`.git` directory** is a hidden folder created when you initialize a Git repository. This folder contains all the internal data Git needs to track and manage your project's version history.

Here's what's inside the `.git` directory:

1. **Objects**: Git stores all your commits, trees (directories), and blobs (file contents) in this directory.
2. **Refs**: This contains pointers to commits, such as branches and tags. It tells Git where the head of each branch is.
3. **Index**: The index is essentially Git's staging area. It tracks changes that are staged but not yet committed.
4. **Logs**: Git maintains logs of all operations performed on the repository, such as commits and merges.

Note: You generally don't need to interact directly with the `.git` directory, as Git handles everything internally. However, understanding its structure helps you appreciate how Git manages your repository and keeps track of your changes.

To view the `.git` directory:

```bash

ls -a
```

You should see the `.git` directory in the list of files. Inside this folder, you'll find various files and subdirectories Git uses to manage the project.

Understanding the Working Directory, Staging Area, and Commit History

Git operates with three primary areas to manage changes: the **working directory**, the **staging area**, and the **commit history**.

1. **Working Directory**:
   - This is where you edit and work with files in your project. Files in the working directory are **untracked** (if they haven't been added to Git) or

modified (if changes have been made since the last commit).

o   When you run `git status`, Git tells you which files are in the working directory and whether they've been modified.

2. **Staging Area (Index)**:

o   The staging area is a temporary place where you can prepare changes before committing them to your Git repository.

o   When you use the `git add` command, Git moves the changes to the staging area.

o   You can stage individual files or all modified files, and only the files in the staging area are included in your next commit.

Example:

```bash
bash

git add index.html
```

3. **Commit History (Local Repository)**:

o   The commit history is where all committed changes are stored. Every time you commit your changes, they're saved in the Git repository, creating a new entry in the history.

o   Git keeps track of every commit, allowing you to view the complete history of your project, roll back to previous versions, and track changes over time.

Example:

```
bash
```

```
git commit -m "Updated homepage content"
```

Real-World Example: Tracking Changes and Viewing History

Let's walk through a real-world example to see how these Git concepts work together.

Imagine you're working on a web development project, and you've made changes to the index.html file. Here's what you would do:

1. **Check the Status**: After making changes to index.html, you can run git status to see which files have been modified:

57

```bash
git status
```

Output:

```bash
On branch master
Changes not staged for commit:
  (use "git add <file>..." to update what
will be committed)
  (use "git restore <file>..." to discard
changes in working directory)
    modified:   index.html
```

2. **Stage the File**: You then decide that you want to keep the changes in index.html, so you stage the file:

```bash
git add index.html
```

3. **Commit the Changes**: After staging the file, you make a commit to record the changes:

```bash
```

```
git commit -m "Added a new header to the
homepage"
```

4. **View the Commit History**: To confirm your changes have been committed, you can view the commit history with `git log`:

bash

```
git log
```

Output:

bash

```
commit
4fbb91d1e6b7b1b5608c9c3cb29f4b4446160b53
Author: Your Name <your_email@example.com>
Date:   Tue Mar 29 14:50:00 2022 -0400

    Added a new header to the homepage

commit
a4b345df5f3d51f5a9b3d85d0fdd3f2e5fbbdbd4
Author: Your Name <your_email@example.com>
Date:   Mon Mar 28 13:43:20 2022 -0400

    Initial commit: added index.html
```

You can now see the commit you just made, with the commit message "Added a new header to the homepage," along with its unique commit ID.

Key Takeaways:

- **git status** helps you track the current state of your repository, showing which files have been modified, staged, or untracked.

- **git log** provides the history of your commits, allowing you to track changes and see who made them.

- The **.git directory** contains all of Git's internal data and metadata for tracking changes.

- **Working Directory**: The location where your files are edited.

- **Staging Area**: The area where changes are prepared before committing.

- **Commit History**: The record of all committed changes in the repository.

By using these commands and understanding the structure of your Git repository, you can efficiently track changes, collaborate with others, and manage your project's version history. In the next chapter, we'll explore how to use **branching** to manage different features or versions of your project.

CHAPTER 5

BRANCHING AND MERGING

In software development, **branching** and **merging** are two of the most important concepts that help you manage code changes and collaborate effectively with team members. Git makes it easy to work with different versions of your project simultaneously, and these powerful features enable you to experiment with new ideas, fix bugs, or develop features in isolation without affecting the main codebase. In this chapter, we'll cover the fundamentals of **branching**, how to create, switch, and delete branches, and how to **merge** them back together. We'll also explore conflict resolution, a common issue that arises during the merging process. Finally, we'll walk through a real-world example of working on features in isolation and then merging them back into the main project.

What are Branches and Why Are They Important?

Branches in Git allow you to create separate environments for developing features, experimenting with changes, or fixing bugs, all without interfering with the main codebase. Instead of modifying the main code directly (usually referred to as the **master** or **main** branch), developers can create a branch to work on a new feature or fix in isolation. Once the work is completed, the branch can be merged back into the main project.

Why Branching Is Important:

1. **Isolated Development**: You can work on new features or bug fixes without affecting the stable version of the project.

2. **Parallel Work**: Multiple developers can work on different features or fixes at the same time without interfering with each other's work.

3. **Experimentation**: If you want to try something new, such as a different approach to solving a problem, branching allows you to experiment safely. If it doesn't work out, you can simply discard the branch.

4. **Versioning**: Branching allows you to maintain multiple versions of your project simultaneously, such as for different stages of development (e.g., a development branch, a testing branch, and a production branch).

Creating, Switching, and Deleting Branches with Git

Let's now look at how to create, switch, and delete branches using Git.

1. **Creating a New Branch**:
    - To create a new branch, use the following command:

    bash

    ```
    git branch <branch_name>
    ```

    - This creates a new branch but doesn't switch to it. You can check the branches in your repository with:

    bash

    ```
    git branch
    ```

    The current branch will be highlighted with an asterisk.

2. **Switching Between Branches**:

- o To switch to an existing branch, use the `git checkout` command:

```bash
git checkout <branch_name>
```

- o As of Git version 2.23, you can use the new `git switch` command, which is more intuitive:

```bash
git switch <branch_name>
```

3. **Creating and Switching to a Branch**:

- o You can create and switch to a new branch in one command by using:

```bash
git checkout -b <branch_name>
```

Or with the `git switch` command:

```bash
git switch -c <branch_name>
```

4. **Deleting a Branch**:

  o Once a branch is no longer needed (for example, after merging the feature into the main branch), you can delete it with:

```bash

git branch -d <branch_name>
```

  The -d flag stands for "delete," and this command will only delete the branch if it has been fully merged. If you want to force delete a branch (e.g., if you haven't merged it yet), you can use:

```bash

git branch -D <branch_name>
```

Merging Branches and Resolving Conflicts

Once you've finished working on a branch and are ready to integrate your changes with the main codebase, you'll need to **merge** the branch back into the branch you want to integrate with (often the main or master branch).

66

1. **Merging Branches**:

   o To merge a branch into your current branch, first, make sure you are on the branch you want to merge into (e.g., `main`):

   bash

   ```
   git checkout main
   ```

   o Then use the `git merge` command:

   bash

   ```
   git merge <branch_name>
   ```

   This merges the changes from the specified branch into your current branch.

2. **Handling Merge Conflicts**:

   o A **merge conflict** occurs when Git can't automatically merge changes from two branches because they modify the same part of a file or have conflicting changes. In this case, Git will highlight the conflict, and you'll need to resolve it manually.

Example of a Merge Conflict:

o Imagine that you and a teammate both made changes to the `index.html` file on different branches. When you try to merge the branches, Git might be unable to merge the two versions automatically if both changes are on the same lines of code.

o Git will mark the conflict within the file with markers like:

bash

```
<<<<<<< HEAD
<code from current branch>
=======
<code from the branch being merged>
>>>>>>> <branch_name>
```

o You'll need to manually edit the file to decide which changes to keep. After resolving the conflict, mark the conflict as resolved by adding the file to the staging area:

bash

```
git add index.html
```

3. Commit the Merge:

- After resolving any conflicts, commit the merge:

```bash
bash
```

```
git commit -m "Merged <branch_name>
into main"
```

Real-World Example: Working on Features in Isolation and Merging Them Back into the Main Project

Let's imagine you're working on a collaborative project, like developing a website, with a team of developers. You're tasked with implementing a new feature: a user authentication system.

1. Create a Branch for the New Feature:

- You begin by creating a new branch called feature/authentication:

```bash
bash
```

```
git            checkout         -b
feature/authentication
```

2. **Work on the Feature in Isolation**:

   o You make changes to files like `auth.js` and `login.html`. As you work, you commit your changes locally:

   bash

   ```
   git add auth.js login.html
   git commit -m "Added authentication
   logic"
   ```

3. **Collaborating with Teammates**:

   o Your teammate is working on a different feature, say the "user profile" page, and creates their own branch, `feature/profile`. They make changes and commit them separately, without interfering with your work on the authentication feature.

   o You can both commit changes, push them to your respective branches, and when ready, merge your work into the main branch.

4. **Merging Your Feature into the Main Branch**:

   o Once the authentication feature is complete, you merge your branch into the `main` branch:

   bash

```
git checkout main
git merge feature/authentication
```

5. **Dealing with Conflicts (if any)**:

   o   Suppose your teammate made changes to the `login.html` file on the `feature/profile` branch, and when you merge your `feature/authentication` branch, you encounter a conflict.

   o   Git will notify you of the conflict, and you will manually resolve it by editing `login.html` and deciding which code to keep.

   o   Once the conflict is resolved, stage the file and commit the merge:

   ```
   bash
   ```

   ```
   git add login.html
   git commit -m "Merged authentication
   feature and resolved conflicts"
   ```

6. **Push the Merged Code to the Remote Repository**:

   o   Finally, push your merged code to the remote repository on GitHub or GitLab:

```bash

git push origin main
```

Key Takeaways:

- **Branches** in Git allow you to work on features, fixes, or experiments in isolation, keeping your main codebase stable.

- You can **create, switch,** and **delete** branches easily with the `git branch` and `git checkout` commands.

- **Merging** integrates changes from one branch into another. Git automatically merges changes when possible but will require manual intervention if there are conflicts.

- **Merge conflicts** occur when changes in two branches conflict, and you'll need to resolve these manually by editing the conflicting files.

- Branching and merging are essential for collaborative workflows, enabling teams to work simultaneously on different parts of a project without interfering with each other's work.

In the next chapter, we'll explore **Git remotes** and learn how to work with remote repositories on platforms like GitHub and GitLab, so you can collaborate with other developers and manage your project online.

CHAPTER 6

UNDERSTANDING GIT REMOTES

In this chapter, we will explore the concept of **Git remotes**, how they differ from local repositories, and the essential operations you can perform to collaborate on a project with remote teams. Working with remotes is a vital part of using Git in modern software development, especially when working in a team. We will also cover how to **clone** a remote repository, and perform the basic operations of **push**, **pull**, and **fetch** to synchronize your work with others.

What Are Remotes? How Do They Differ from Local Repositories?

A **remote repository** in Git is a version of your project that is hosted on a remote server, typically in the cloud (e.g., GitHub, GitLab, or Bitbucket). It's where all developers can share their work and collaborate in a central location. Remotes are particularly useful for teams, allowing multiple people to work on the same project simultaneously without overwriting each other's changes.

In contrast, a **local repository** exists on your own computer. It holds all the files and history of the project, and is used for working on your code. Each developer has their own local of the repository, and changes are first made locally before being shared with others.

Key Differences:

- **Local Repository**: Exists on your local machine. You can make commits, create branches, and work offline. It's your personal version of the project.
- **Remote Repository**: A shared version of the repository hosted on a remote server. It's where multiple developers can push and pull changes to collaborate.

To interact with the remote repository, you will need to link it to your local repository using the **remote URL**.

Cloning a Remote Repository and Working with It Locally

When you want to collaborate on a project, the first step is usually to clone the repository. Cloning creates a of the remote repository on your local machine, allowing you to make changes locally and then sync those changes with others.

Cloning a Remote Repository: To clone a remote repository, use the `git clone` command followed by the URL of the remote repository:

bash

```
git                                             clone
https://github.com/username/repository-name.git
```

This command does several things:

1. It creates a directory on your local machine with the repository's name.
2. It downloads the entire repository, including its history, branches, and files.
3. It automatically sets up a **remote link** to the original repository so that you can fetch, pull, and push changes later.

Once the repository is cloned, navigate into the project directory:

bash

```
cd repository-name
```

Now, you can work with the repository as if it were a local one. Any changes you make can be committed locally and then pushed to the remote when you're ready.

Push, Pull, and Fetch Operations

Git provides three main operations for syncing your local repository with a remote repository: **push**, **pull**, and **fetch**. These operations are essential for working in a team, as they allow you to share and retrieve changes from others.

1. **git push**:
   - The `git push` command is used to upload your local commits to a remote repository. When you push changes, you're essentially sending your local commits to the remote repository so that other developers can access them.
   - Example:

   ```bash
   git push origin main
   ```

77

This pushes your changes from the local `main` branch to the remote `main` branch on the server named `origin` (which is the default name for the remote repository).

2. **git pull**:

   o The `git pull` command is used to download changes from the remote repository and merge them into your local repository. This operation combines `git fetch` and `git merge` into one step.

   o Example:

   ```bash
   git pull origin main
   ```

   This fetches the latest changes from the remote `main` branch and merges them into your local `main` branch.

3. **git fetch**:

   o The `git fetch` command retrieves the latest changes from the remote repository but does not merge them into your local repository. This allows you to see the updates before deciding how to integrate them.

o   Example:

```
bash
```

```
git fetch origin
```

This command fetches all branches from the remote repository but leaves your local branches untouched. After fetching, you can inspect the changes using `git log` and decide how to integrate them.

Real-World Example: Collaborating on a Project with Remote Teams

Let's walk through a real-world example where you're collaborating on a project with a team of developers using a remote repository on **GitHub**.

Step 1: Clone the Remote Repository
You're working on a **web application** project with a team. Your

colleague has already created a remote repository on GitHub, and you need to clone it to get started.

To clone the repository, you use the following command:

```bash
```

```
git clone https://github.com/team-name/web-app.git
```

After cloning, you have a full local of the repository on your computer. You can now navigate to the project directory:

```bash
```

```
cd web-app
```

Step 2: Create a New Branch for Your Feature

You're assigned to add a new feature to the website. To work on the feature, you create a new branch from `main`:

```bash
```

```
git checkout -b feature/user-login
```

You make changes to the project's `login.html` and `login.js` files.

Step 3: Stage and Commit Your Changes

After completing your changes, you stage the modified files:

```bash
git add login.html login.js
```

Then, you commit the changes with a meaningful commit message:

```bash
git commit -m "Added user login form"
```

Step 4: Push Your Changes to the Remote Repository

Once you've committed your changes, it's time to push them to the remote repository so that your teammates can review and merge them. You push your branch to the remote:

```bash
git push origin feature/user-login
```

Step 5: Create a Pull Request

After pushing your changes to GitHub, you go to the repository's page on GitHub and open a **pull request**. A pull request is a request to merge your branch into the main project branch (usually `main` or `master`), where your teammates can review your changes, leave comments, and merge them if everything looks good.

Step 6: Pull Changes from the Remote Repository
Meanwhile, other developers have made changes to the `main` branch, and you want to make sure your local repository is up to date before continuing your work.

You run the `git pull` command to fetch and merge the changes from the remote `main` branch into your local repository:

```bash

git pull origin main
```

If there are no merge conflicts, your local repository is now up to date with the remote. If there are conflicts, Git will alert you, and you can resolve them manually.

Step 7: Collaborating and Merging the Pull Request
Once your pull request has been reviewed and approved, it's merged into the `main` branch by one of your teammates. The feature is now part of the main project!

Step 8: Keeping Your Local Repository Up-to-Date

After the merge, you run `git pull` again to ensure that your local repository reflects the latest changes in the remote repository:

bash

git pull origin main

This ensures you have the most up-to-date version of the project, and you're ready to start working on the next task.

Key Takeaways:

- **Git remotes** are repositories hosted on a remote server that allow developers to collaborate and share their work.
- You can **clone** a remote repository to get a of the project on your local machine.
- **Push** uploads your changes from your local repository to the remote, and **pull** downloads changes from the remote to your local repository.
- **Fetch** retrieves the latest changes from the remote without merging them, giving you a chance to review changes before integrating them.

- **Branching** allows you to work on new features or fixes in isolation without affecting the main project.

- Using **Git remotes** and collaborating on platforms like **GitHub** or **GitLab** helps you work efficiently with remote teams, keeping everyone in sync.

In the next chapter, we'll explore **rebasing**, an advanced technique for keeping your feature branches up to date with the latest changes in the main branch without creating unnecessary merge commits.

CHAPTER 7

REBASING: UNDERSTANDING

AND USING IT

In Git, **rebasing** is a powerful technique for integrating changes from one branch into another. Unlike merging, which creates a new commit to combine changes, rebasing rewrites the commit history to create a linear progression of changes. This chapter will introduce you to **rebasing**, explain when and why you should use it, compare it to **merging**, and walk you through a real-world example of how rebasing helps keep a project history clean.

What is Rebasing and When Should You Use It?

Rebasing is the process of moving or "replaying" commits from one branch onto another. It allows you to take the changes from one branch and apply them on top of another branch, essentially creating a **linear history**.

When you rebase, Git:

1. Takes each commit in your current branch and **removes** them temporarily.

2. Applies the latest changes from the base branch (usually `main` or `master`).

3. Re-applies your commits **one by one** on top of the updated base branch.

The result is a branch with a clean, linear commit history, which can make it easier to understand the progression of changes. Rebasing is particularly useful when you want to:

- Incorporate the latest changes from the main branch into your feature branch without creating a **merge commit**.
- Keep the history **clean** and easy to follow.

When should you use rebasing?

- **Before merging your feature branch** into the main branch to avoid unnecessary merge commits and keep the history linear.
- **To update your feature branch** with the latest changes from the main branch, especially if your feature branch has diverged significantly.

- **When working in teams,** to ensure everyone is working with the latest code without cluttering the commit history with merge commits.

However, rebasing is a more **advanced operation** that should be used carefully, especially with shared branches. Rebasing rewrites commit history, which can lead to problems if not done correctly.

Rebase vs. Merge: Key Differences and Use Cases

Both **rebasing** and **merging** are ways to integrate changes from one branch into another, but they do so in different ways.

Feature	Rebasing	Merging
Commit History	Creates a linear history, no merge commits	Creates a non-linear history with merge commits
How Changes are Integrated	Moves or "replays" commits from one branch onto another	Combines the changes in two branches with a merge commit

Feature	Rebasing	Merging
Ease of Understanding	Clean, easy-to-follow history without merge commits	Can result in a more complicated history with multiple merge commits
Risk of Conflicts	Can be more prone to conflicts, especially with rebasing shared branches	Conflicts can arise during the merge process, but the history remains intact
Ideal Use Case	Keeping a branch up-to-date with the latest changes, maintaining a clean history	Keeping track of when branches were merged and preserving all changes
When to Use	Before merging into main branch, when working on long-lived feature branches	For major features, collaborative work, or preserving the full history

When to use Rebase:

- You are working on a feature branch and want to ensure that your work is applied on top of the latest version of the `main` branch.

- You want to maintain a clean, linear history without merge commits.

When to use Merge:

- You are collaborating with others on a shared branch, where preserving the complete history (including when merges happened) is important.

- You want to maintain the integrity of your project history, showing exactly when and how different features were integrated.

Real-World Example: Keeping a Clean Project History with Rebasing

Let's walk through an example of **rebasing** in a real-world scenario where you're working on a feature branch and want to keep the project history clean while incorporating the latest changes from the `main` branch.

Scenario:

You're working on a **feature branch** called `feature/authentication` to add a user authentication system to the project. Meanwhile, the `main` branch has received several updates from other team members, and you need to update your branch with the latest changes.

1. **Your Current Setup**:
   - You have the `main` branch, which is up-to-date with the latest changes.
   - You have a `feature/authentication` branch, which was created from the `main` branch some time ago, and now has diverged from it.
   - You want to incorporate the changes from `main` into your `feature/authentication` branch to avoid potential merge conflicts when you eventually merge your feature back into `main`.

2. **Step 1: Checkout to Your Feature Branch**: First, ensure you are on your `feature/authentication` branch:

```bash
git checkout feature/authentication
```

3. **Step 2: Fetch the Latest Changes**: Fetch the latest changes from the remote repository (without merging them yet):

bash

```
git fetch origin
```

4. **Step 3: Rebase Your Feature Branch onto main**: Now, rebase your `feature/authentication` branch onto the latest version of `main`. This will effectively move your commits from `feature/authentication` on top of the updated `main` branch:

bash

```
git rebase origin/main
```

Git will go through each commit in your branch, apply the latest changes from the `main` branch, and replay your commits on top of them.

5. **Step 4: Resolving Conflicts**: If there are conflicts during the rebase (e.g., changes in `index.html` that overlap), Git will pause the rebase and prompt you to resolve the conflicts manually. You can open the conflicted files and resolve the issues. After resolving conflicts:

91

```
bash
```

```
git add <conflicted-file>
git rebase --continue
```

Repeat this process until all conflicts are resolved and the rebase is complete.

6. **Step 5: Verify the Rebase**: After the rebase is finished, you can view the commit history to ensure your feature branch has the latest changes from main:

```
bash
```

```
git log --oneline --graph
```

7. **Step 6: Push Your Changes**: After rebasing, you may need to force-push your branch to the remote repository (since rebasing rewrites commit history):

```
bash
```

```
git push origin feature/authentication --
force
```

8. **Step 7: Create a Pull Request**: Now that your feature branch is up-to-date with the latest changes from main,

you can create a pull request to merge your feature/authentication branch into main. Since you've rebased, this merge will have a clean, linear history without extra merge commits.

Key Takeaways:

- **Rebasing** allows you to maintain a clean, linear project history by moving your commits on top of the latest changes from another branch (typically main).

- **Rebase vs. Merge**: Use **rebase** to keep a tidy history, especially for individual feature branches. Use **merge** when collaborating with others and preserving the full history of changes is important.

- **Rebase Workflow**: You fetch the latest changes from the remote, rebase your feature branch onto main, resolve any conflicts, and then push the updated branch to the remote repository.

- **When to use rebase**: Use it to keep your branch up-to-date with main before merging, to avoid unnecessary merge commits, and to maintain a clean and linear history.

In the next chapter, we will dive into **cherry-picking commits**, an advanced technique that allows you to apply individual commits from one branch to another, which is useful when you need to apply specific changes across multiple branches.

CHAPTER 8

CHERRY-PICKING COMMITS

In Git, the concept of **cherry-picking** allows you to select individual commits from one branch and apply them to another branch. This can be extremely useful when you want to apply specific changes from a feature branch or bug fix without merging the entire branch. Cherry-picking provides fine-grained control over what changes you introduce into your project.

In this chapter, we will cover the **concept of cherry-picking**, how to apply specific commits to your branch using Git, and provide a **real-world example** of using cherry-picking to fix bugs in multiple branches.

Understanding the Concept of Cherry-picking in Git

Cherry-picking is the process of applying a single commit (or a range of commits) from one branch to another. This allows you to selectively specific changes without merging the entire branch or its history. Essentially, cherry-picking lets you **pick and apply**

95

changes from one branch onto another without having to merge all the other changes that might not be relevant.

Cherry-picking is particularly useful in the following scenarios:

- **Bug Fixes**: You've fixed a bug on one branch and want to apply the same fix to another branch.
- **Feature Updates**: You need to pull specific changes or improvements from a feature branch into your main development branch.
- **Selective Changes**: When you don't want to merge an entire branch but only need a particular commit or set of commits.

How to Apply Specific Commits to Your Branch

The basic syntax for cherry-picking a commit in Git is:

```bash
```

```
git cherry-pick <commit_hash>
```

Where <commit_hash> is the unique identifier for the commit you want to apply. You can find the commit hash using git log.

1. **Finding the Commit Hash**:

   o First, use `git log` to find the commit hash of the commit you want to cherry-pick:

   ```bash
   ```

   ```bash
   git log
   ```

   o You will see a list of commits with their commit hashes (the long alphanumeric strings). For example:

   ```bash
   ```

   ```bash
   commit
   f4b9d3c7cbb1a98b7bbfc83a9f43b658dd9
   ed232
   Author:          Your          Name
   <your_email@example.com>
   Date:    Mon Mar 29 13:25:40 2022 -
   0400

       Fixed bug in user authentication
   ```

2. **Cherry-picking the Commit**: Once you have the commit hash, you can cherry-pick that commit into your current branch:

```bash
bash
```

```bash
git                        cherry-pick
f4b9d3c7cbb1a98b7bbfc83a9f43b658dd9ed232
```

This command will apply the changes from that commit onto your current branch.

3. **Cherry-picking Multiple Commits**: You can also cherry-pick a range of commits by specifying a commit range:

```bash
bash
```

```bash
git                        cherry-pick
<commit_hash1>^..<commit_hash2>
```

The caret (^) indicates the commit before the first commit in the range, so both commits and all changes in between are included.

4. **Resolving Conflicts**: If the cherry-pick operation causes a conflict (e.g., the changes in the commit conflict with the changes in your current branch), Git will pause the cherry-pick and allow you to resolve the conflict manually.

After resolving the conflict, stage the changes:

```bash
git add <conflicted-file>
```

Then, continue the cherry-pick:

```bash
git cherry-pick --continue
```

If you want to abort the cherry-pick process, use:

```bash
git cherry-pick --abort
```

Real-World Example: Fixing Bugs in Multiple Branches by Cherry-picking Commits

Let's go through a real-world example where cherry-picking is used to fix a bug in multiple branches.

Scenario:

You're working on an e-commerce website with two active branches: `main` and `feature/checkout`. You've recently fixed a bug in the `checkout.js` file in the `main` branch, but now you need to apply the same fix to the `feature/checkout` branch, which is based on an older version of `main`.

1. **Step 1: Fix the Bug in the `main` Branch**:

    o   You find a bug in `checkout.js` and fix it in the `main` branch. After making the changes, you commit the fix:

        bash

        ```
        git commit -m "Fixed bug in checkout
        logic"
        ```

2. **Step 2: Find the Commit Hash**:

    o   After the commit, you use `git log` to find the commit hash of the fix:

        bash

        ```
        git log
        ```

        Example output:

        bash

100

```
commit
f4b9d3c7cbb1a98b7bbfc83a9f43b658dd9
ed232
Author:          Your          Name
<your_email@example.com>
Date:     Mon Mar 29 13:25:40 2022 -
0400
```

```
Fixed bug in checkout logic
```

3. **Step 3: Checkout to the `feature/checkout` Branch**:

   o You now switch to the `feature/checkout` branch to apply the fix there:

   ```bash
   bash
   ```

   ```
   git checkout feature/checkout
   ```

4. **Step 4: Cherry-pick the Commit from `main`**:

   o To apply the fix to the `feature/checkout` branch, you cherry-pick the commit from `main`:

   ```bash
   bash
   ```

   ```
   git                    cherry-pick
   f4b9d3c7cbb1a98b7bbfc83a9f43b658dd9
   ed232
   ```

5. **Step 5: Resolve Conflicts (If Any):**

   o Suppose there's a conflict because `checkout.js` was modified in both branches. Git will stop the cherry-pick and prompt you to resolve the conflict.

   o You open `checkout.js` and manually fix the conflict, then stage the file:

   ```bash
   git add checkout.js
   ```

6. **Step 6: Complete the Cherry-pick:**

   o After resolving any conflicts, continue the cherry-pick:

   ```bash
   git cherry-pick --continue
   ```

7. **Step 7: Commit the Changes:**

   o Once the cherry-pick is complete, the changes are committed to the `feature/checkout` branch.

    o You can now push the updated feature/checkout branch to the remote repository:

```bash
git push origin feature/checkout
```

8. **Step 8: Testing and Merging**:

    o Finally, you test the changes in the feature/checkout branch and ensure that the bug fix works as expected. Once everything is confirmed, you can create a pull request to merge the feature/checkout branch back into main.

Key Takeaways:

- **Cherry-picking** allows you to apply specific commits from one branch to another without merging entire branches.

- Use **git cherry-pick <commit_hash>** to apply a single commit, and **git cherry-pick <commit_hash1>^..<commit_hash2>** to apply a range of commits.

- Cherry-picking is ideal for **selective changes**, such as applying a bug fix or feature update to multiple branches.

- When conflicts occur during cherry-picking, Git will stop and ask you to resolve them manually before continuing the process.

- **Real-world use case**: Cherry-picking is often used to apply bug fixes or specific changes from one branch to others without merging the entire branch, keeping the project's history clean and focused.

In the next chapter, we'll explore **stashing changes** in Git, which is useful for saving work temporarily when you need to switch tasks or branches without committing changes.

CHAPTER 9

STASHING CHANGES

In Git, one of the most common challenges developers face is needing to switch tasks quickly or experiment with new ideas without losing their progress. This is where **Git stash** comes into play. Stashing allows you to save your uncommitted changes temporarily and revert your working directory to a clean state, making it easy to switch branches or focus on something else. Once you're ready to resume, you can apply the stashed changes back to your working directory. This chapter will explore **what Git stash is**, **how it works**, and **how to use it effectively** with real-world examples.

What is Git Stash and Why is it Useful?

Git stash is a Git feature that temporarily saves changes in your working directory and staging area. Think of it like putting your changes in a "temporary holding area" so you can return to a clean state in your project. It allows you to:

105

- **Switch branches** without having to commit incomplete or experimental work.

- **Test different changes** or ideas without worrying about losing your current progress.

- **Clean up your working directory** for a quick task, like pulling updates from a remote repository or fixing a critical issue, then resume your work later.

Git stash is particularly useful when:

- You are in the middle of working on a feature but need to switch to another branch to handle an urgent bug or task.

- You want to quickly save and discard changes to your working directory, so you can work on a different task temporarily.

- You want to clean up your working directory before switching branches or before pulling the latest changes from a remote repository.

Saving and Applying Stashed Changes

The **Git stash** command allows you to save your uncommitted changes, including modifications to both tracked and untracked files.

1. **Stashing Changes**:

    o To stash changes in Git, use the following command:

    ```bash
    git stash
    ```

    This will save both your modified tracked files and staged changes (those added to the staging area) while reverting your working directory to the state of the last commit.

    o If you want to include untracked files (files that are not yet added to the Git index), use the -u option:

    ```bash
    git stash -u
    ```

107

This will stash changes in both tracked and untracked files.

o   You can also provide a descriptive message for the stash:

```bash
```

```
git stash save "WIP: Added login form
to homepage"
```

2. **Listing Stashed Changes**:

o   To view the list of all stashed changes, you can use:

```bash
```

```
git stash list
```

This will display all stashed changes in a list, each identified by a stash identifier (e.g., stash@{0}, stash@{1}, etc.).

o   Example output:

```bash
```

```
stash@{0}:              WIP           on
feature/authentication:      1a2b3c4d
Added login form
stash@{1}: WIP  on  feature/payment:
5d6e7f8g Fixed payment bug
```

3. **Applying Stashed Changes**:

    o To apply your most recent stash back to your working directory, use:

    bash

    ```
    git stash apply
    ```

    This applies the changes from the most recent stash without removing it from the stash list.

    o If you want to apply a specific stash, reference its identifier:

    bash

    ```
    git stash apply stash@{1}
    ```

4. **Dropping Stashed Changes**:

- o After applying a stash, it is still stored in your stash list. If you no longer need it, you can remove it with:

  bash

  ```
  git stash drop stash@{1}
  ```

- o To drop the most recent stash, simply use:

  bash

  ```
  git stash drop
  ```

5. **Popping Stashed Changes**:

  - o If you want to apply the changes and remove the stash from the list in one step, use the `git stash pop` command:

    bash

    ```
    git stash pop
    ```

    This applies the most recent stash and removes it from the stash list.

Real-World Example: Saving Work Temporarily and Switching Branches Without Losing Progress

Let's consider a real-world example where you are working on a new feature but need to switch to another branch to handle a critical bug fix, then come back to your work without losing progress.

Scenario:

You're developing a new **user authentication feature** in a branch called `feature/authentication`. You're in the middle of coding the login form, but you get a message that there's a critical bug in the `main` branch related to the payment system that needs to be fixed immediately.

Step 1: Save Your Changes Using Git Stash

You don't want to commit your work yet since it's incomplete. Instead, you can stash your changes:

```bash
bash
```

```bash
git stash
```

Your changes are now saved temporarily, and your working directory is clean.

111

Step 2: Switch to the Bug Fix Branch

Now that your changes are safely stashed, you can switch to the `main` branch and work on fixing the bug:

bash

```
git checkout main
```

Step 3: Fix the Bug and Commit

You fix the bug in the payment system, then commit and push the changes to the remote repository:

bash

```
git add payment.js
git commit -m "Fixed bug in payment system"
git push origin main
```

Step 4: Return to Your Feature Branch

After addressing the critical bug, you switch back to your feature branch:

bash

```
git checkout feature/authentication
```

Step 5: Apply Your Stashed Changes

Now, you can apply the changes you stashed earlier to resume working on your authentication feature:

```bash
git stash apply
```

If you're sure you no longer need the stash, you can use `git stash pop` to apply the changes and remove the stash from the list:

```bash
git stash pop
```

Step 6: Continue Working on the Feature

With the bug fix out of the way and your previous work restored, you can continue working on your authentication feature without losing any progress.

Key Takeaways:

- **Git stash** allows you to save uncommitted changes temporarily and switch tasks or branches without committing incomplete work.

- You can stash both modified and untracked files using `git stash`, and you can retrieve them later with `git stash apply` or `git stash pop`.

- Stashing is particularly useful when you need to switch branches or tackle another task temporarily, without committing unfinished work.

- **Popping** a stash applies the changes and removes the stash, while **applying** a stash keeps it in the list for later use.

- **Real-world use case**: Stashing allows you to manage multiple tasks simultaneously—such as fixing urgent bugs—without losing progress on ongoing work.

In the next chapter, we'll explore **Git tags**, a useful feature for marking specific points in your project's history, such as releases or milestones, making it easier to refer to those versions later.

CHAPTER 10

WORKING WITH TAGS

In Git, **tags** are used to mark specific points in the commit history, making it easy to refer to particular versions of your project. Tags are commonly used to mark **releases, milestones,** or **important events** in the development lifecycle. Tags allow you to easily access specific points in your project's history without having to remember commit hashes or use logs.

In this chapter, we'll explore what **tags** are in Git, how to create **lightweight** and **annotated** tags, and provide a **real-world example** of using tags to mark specific points in your project, such as software releases.

What Are Tags in Git and How Are They Used?

A **tag** in Git is essentially a reference to a specific commit. It's a way to label a commit with a user-friendly name, so you can easily reference it later. Tags are often used for marking release versions (e.g., `v1.0`, `v2.0`) or important milestones in your project.

Why Use Tags?

- **Releases**: Tags are commonly used to mark release points in the project, such as version 1.0, 2.0, etc.

- **Milestones**: Tags can be used to mark milestones in the development process, such as "feature complete," "beta," or "production."

- **Reference Points**: Tags provide a way to easily reference important points in the history of your project without needing to remember commit hashes.

There are two types of tags in Git:

1. **Lightweight tags**
2. **Annotated tags**

Creating Lightweight and Annotated Tags

1. **Lightweight Tags**:
   - A **lightweight tag** is like a simple pointer to a specific commit. It is just a reference to a commit and does not contain any additional information (such as the tagger's name, email, or date).

o Lightweight tags are useful for quick references or temporary markers. They don't have any extra metadata.

Creating a Lightweight Tag: To create a lightweight tag, use the following command:

bash

```
git tag <tag_name>
```

For example, if you want to create a tag named v1.0 to mark your first version:

bash

```
git tag v1.0
```

2. **Annotated Tags**:

o An **annotated tag** contains more information, such as the tagger's name, email, date, and a tagging message. Annotated tags are stored as full objects in the Git database and are recommended for marking important versions, like releases.

o   Annotated tags are useful when you want to keep track of who created the tag and why it was created.

Creating an Annotated Tag: To create an annotated tag, use the following command:

bash

```
git tag -a <tag_name> -m "Tagging version
1.0"
```

For example, to create an annotated tag named v1.0 with a message:

bash

```
git tag -a v1.0 -m "Version 1.0 - Initial
Release"
```

This creates a tag with a message, and you can view the tag's information using:

bash

```
git show v1.0
```

Viewing, Pushing, and Deleting Tags

1. **Viewing Tags**:

   o To see all the tags in your repository, run:

   ```bash
   git tag
   ```

   o This will display all tags in alphabetical order.

2. **Pushing Tags to a Remote Repository**:

   o By default, tags are not automatically pushed to the remote repository when you use `git push`. To push a specific tag, use:

   ```bash
   git push origin <tag_name>
   ```

   o To push all tags at once, use:

   ```bash
   git push --tags
   ```

3. **Deleting Tags**:

   o To delete a tag locally, use:

```bash
git tag -d <tag_name>
```

o   To delete a tag from the remote repository, use:

```bash
git push origin --delete tag <tag_name>
```

Real-World Example: Marking Specific Points in Your Project, Such as Releases

Let's walk through a real-world example where you use tags to mark software releases in a project.

Scenario:

You're working on a software project and want to release version 1.0. You've completed the development work and are ready to mark the release point.

1. **Step 1: Ensure You Are on the Correct Commit**: First, make sure you are on the correct commit that represents the state of the project for version 1.0:

```bash

git checkout main
```

2. **Step 2: Create an Annotated Tag for Version 1.0**: Create an annotated tag to mark the release:

```bash

git tag -a v1.0 -m "Version 1.0 - Initial Release"
```

3. **Step 3: Push the Tag to the Remote Repository**: After creating the tag locally, push it to your remote repository (e.g., on GitHub or GitLab):

```bash

git push origin v1.0
```

4. **Step 4: View the Tag Information**: To view the details of the tag (including the commit and tag message), use:

```bash

git show v1.0
```

This will display the commit details along with the tag message.

5. **Step 5: Creating a Tag for a Future Release**: Let's say you've finished implementing version 1.1, and you're ready to release it. You would follow a similar process:

bash

```
git tag -a v1.1 -m "Version 1.1 - Bug Fixes
and Performance Improvements"
git push origin v1.1
```

6. **Step 6: Using Tags to Checkout Specific Versions**: Tags are helpful when you want to go back to a specific release. For example, if you need to check out version 1.0 to work on a patch or to investigate an issue, you can do so by checking out the tag:

bash

```
git checkout v1.0
```

This will move you to the commit that was tagged as v1.0.

Key Takeaways:

- **Tags** in Git allow you to mark specific points in your project history, such as releases or milestones, making it easier to refer to those versions later.

- There are two types of tags:

  o **Lightweight tags**: Simple references to commits with no additional metadata.

  o **Annotated tags**: Tags with metadata, including the tagger's name, email, date, and a commit message.

- To **view tags**, use `git tag`; to **push tags** to a remote repository, use `git push origin <tag_name>` or `git push --tags` for all tags.

- Tags are ideal for marking **releases** and **milestones**, allowing you to easily navigate and refer to specific versions of your project.

Tags are a simple yet powerful way to keep track of important versions of your project. In the next chapter, we will explore **Git workflows** in more detail, including popular strategies for branching and collaborating with teams effectively.

CHAPTER 11

FORKING AND CLONING REPOSITORIES

Collaboration is at the heart of modern software development, and Git provides robust tools for teams to work together efficiently. Two of the most common ways to collaborate on a project are **forking** and **cloning** repositories. In this chapter, we'll explore the differences between **forking** and **cloning**, when and why you should fork a project, and how to make changes to someone else's repository. We'll also walk through a **real-world example** of contributing to an **open-source project** by forking and cloning repositories.

Difference Between Forking and Cloning

Although both **forking** and **cloning** are ways of obtaining a of a repository, they serve different purposes and are used in different scenarios.

1. **Cloning**:

o **Cloning** is the process of creating a local of an entire remote repository. When you clone a repository, you get a full of the project, including all of its branches, history, and files.

o Cloning is typically used when you want to work on a project **locally**. It gives you full access to the repository, allowing you to make changes, create branches, and commit locally. However, **cloning** does not create a connection between your local and the original project in the sense that it doesn't create a way to contribute back directly unless you have push access to the remote repository.

Command to clone a repository:

```bash
git                                    clone
https://github.com/username/repository-
name.git
```

2. **Forking:**

o **Forking** is used primarily in collaborative or open-source environments. When you **fork** a repository, you create a **personal** of someone else's repository on your GitHub (or other Git hosting service) account. This enables you to experiment with changes freely without affecting the original repository.

o Forking is typically used when you want to contribute to someone else's project, as it allows you to propose changes (via **pull requests**) without needing direct write access to the original repository. After forking, you can clone your fork to work locally and then push changes to your forked repository.

Forking a repository:

o Go to the GitHub page of the repository you want to contribute to.

o Click the **Fork** button in the top-right corner of the page.

o This will create a of the repository in your own GitHub account, where you can freely make changes.

When to Fork a Project and How to Make Changes to Someone Else's Repository

Forking is a common workflow in **open-source development**, where contributors do not have direct access to the original repository. Instead, they fork the repository to their account, make changes, and then submit those changes as a **pull request** for the repository maintainers to review.

Here's when you should consider forking:

- You want to contribute to an open-source project or collaborate on a project that you don't own.
- You need to experiment with changes without affecting the original repository.
- You want to propose features or bug fixes to someone else's repository.

Steps to Fork and Contribute to a Repository:

1. **Fork the Repository:**
   o Navigate to the repository you want to contribute to (e.g., an open-source project).

128

- o Click on the **Fork** button on GitHub (or the equivalent button on other platforms like GitLab).
- o This will create a of the repository in your GitHub account.

2. **Clone the Forked Repository**:

- o After forking the repository, you need to **clone** it to your local machine in order to work on it.
- o the URL of your forked repository from GitHub (e.g., `https://github.com/your-username/repository-name.git`).
- o Run the following command to clone your forked repository:

```bash

git clone https://github.com/your-username/repository-name.git
```

3. **Create a New Branch**:

- o It's best practice to create a new branch for the feature or bug fix you are working on, rather than directly committing to the `main` branch.
- o Example:

```
bash
```

```
git checkout -b feature/your-feature
```

4. **Make Changes Locally**:

   o Now, make the necessary changes to the project in your local repository. You can add new features, fix bugs, or improve documentation.

5. **Commit Your Changes**:

   o Once you've made your changes, commit them to your local repository:

```
bash
```

```
git add .
git commit -m "Your commit message
describing the changes"
```

6. **Push Changes to Your Fork**:

   o After committing the changes, you need to push them to your forked repository on GitHub:

```
bash
```

```
git push origin feature/your-feature
```

7. **Create a Pull Request (PR)**:

- o Once your changes are pushed to your fork, you can submit a **pull request** to the original repository. This allows the maintainers of the original project to review your changes.

- o On GitHub, navigate to your forked repository and click on the **Compare & Pull Request** button. Provide a description of the changes and submit the pull request.

- o If the project maintainers accept your pull request, they will merge your changes into the original repository.

Real-World Example: Contributing to Open-Source Projects

Let's walk through a real-world example of contributing to an open-source project, such as a popular library or framework.

Scenario:

You want to contribute to an open-source library for data visualization, and you've found a bug in the library's code. You want to fix the bug and submit a pull request.

1. **Fork the Repository**:

- Navigate to the open-source project's GitHub page, such as `https://github.com/username/data-viz-lib`.

- Click the **Fork** button in the top-right corner of the page to create a of the repository in your GitHub account.

2. **Clone Your Fork:**

- the URL of your forked repository (e.g., `https://github.com/your-username/data-viz-lib.git`).

- Clone the repository to your local machine:

```bash
```

```
git clone https://github.com/your-username/data-viz-lib.git
cd data-viz-lib
```

3. **Create a New Branch:**

- Create a new branch for the bug fix you will be working on:

```bash
```

```
git checkout -b bugfix/fix-chart-
legend
```

4. **Fix the Bug**:

   o You locate and fix the bug in the code (for example, fixing a broken chart legend).

   o After making the fix, you test it locally to ensure the bug is resolved.

5. **Commit and Push the Changes**:

   o Add and commit your changes:

   ```bash
   ```

   ```
   git add legend.js
   git commit -m "Fixed bug with chart legend not displaying"
   ```

   o Push the changes to your fork:

   ```bash
   ```

   ```
   git push origin bugfix/fix-chart-
   legend
   ```

6. **Submit a Pull Request**:

   o Go to your fork on GitHub, and you'll see an option to create a pull request.

133

- o Click **Compare & Pull Request**, provide a clear description of the bug fix, and submit the pull request to the original repository.

7. **Wait for Review**:

- o The repository maintainers will review your pull request. If everything looks good, they will merge your changes into the main project.

Key Takeaways:

- **Cloning** is the process of creating a local of a repository to work on it, while **forking** is creating a personal of someone else's repository on your GitHub account.

- Forking is ideal for contributing to open-source projects or when you don't have direct access to the original repository.

- After forking a repository, you **clone** it to your local machine, **create a branch**, make changes, **commit** those changes, and **push** them to your fork.

- Once your changes are pushed to your fork, you can submit a **pull request** to the original repository for the maintainers to review and merge.

- Forking and cloning allow for **collaborative work** on open-source and team projects without directly modifying the original codebase.

In the next chapter, we will discuss **Git workflows**, which are strategies and best practices for managing branches, pull requests, and merges in collaborative projects.

CHAPTER 12

PULL REQUESTS AND CODE REVIEWS

A **pull request (PR)** is a key component of collaborative software development. It's a way of proposing changes to a project, allowing others to review and discuss the modifications before they are integrated into the main codebase. In this chapter, we will dive into what a **pull request** is, how to create one, and best practices for both **submitting** and **reviewing** pull requests. We'll also walk through a **real-world example** of managing code reviews and incorporating feedback, which is critical for maintaining high-quality code in a collaborative environment.

What is a Pull Request and How to Create One?

A **pull request** is a mechanism for requesting that changes from a **feature branch** (or any other branch) be merged into the **main branch** or another target branch. When you create a pull request, you are notifying project maintainers or collaborators that you have completed a set of changes and are ready for them to be reviewed and merged into the main codebase.

Key Features of a Pull Request:

- **Propose changes**: A pull request proposes changes made on a feature branch or fork to be merged into the target branch (e.g., `main` or `develop`).

- **Review and discussion**: It serves as a discussion platform for collaborators to review, comment, and suggest improvements on the proposed changes before they are merged.

- **Code Quality**: It helps maintain high code quality through peer reviews, ensuring that the changes meet project standards and that bugs or issues are caught early.

How to Create a Pull Request:

1. **Step 1: Commit and Push Your Changes**:
   - First, ensure you have committed all your changes locally and pushed them to your remote repository (on GitHub, GitLab, etc.). For example:

```
bash

git add .
git commit -m "Implemented user
authentication feature"
git           push           origin
feature/authentication
```

2. **Step 2: Navigate to the Repository's Pull Request Section:**

   o Go to the repository's page on GitHub (or GitLab, Bitbucket, etc.), and find the **Pull Requests** tab.

   o Click the **New Pull Request** button to begin the process.

3. **Step 3: Select the Branches to Compare:**

   o Select the **base branch** (usually `main` or `develop`) and the **compare branch** (the branch you made changes in, such as `feature/authentication`).

   o GitHub will automatically show you the changes made in the compare branch relative to the base branch.

4. **Step 4: Add a Title and Description:**

138

- o Provide a clear **title** and detailed **description** of the pull request. The description should explain the purpose of the changes, the problem being solved, and any important context or considerations.
- o For example:

```
sql

Title: Added User Authentication
Feature

Description: This pull request
implements a user authentication
feature using JWT tokens. It
includes:
- User login API endpoint
- JWT token generation and validation
- Frontend form for logging in users

Please review and let me know if any
changes are needed.
```

5. **Step 5: Create the Pull Request**:

- o Once everything looks good, click the **Create Pull Request** button.

139

o Your pull request is now created, and collaborators can begin reviewing it.

Best Practices for Submitting and Reviewing Pull Requests

1. **Best Practices for Submitting Pull Requests**:

   o **Work in Small, Focused Pull Requests**: Keep pull requests small and focused on a single change or feature. Avoid bundling unrelated changes in a single pull request to make it easier for reviewers to focus on specific aspects of the change.

   o **Provide a Descriptive Title and Description**: The pull request title and description should clearly explain the purpose of the changes and any specific areas of concern or special instructions. This helps reviewers understand the context and scope of the changes.

   o **Follow Code Standards**: Ensure that your code follows the project's coding style and guidelines. This makes it easier for reviewers to understand the code and ensures consistency across the project.

o **Test Your Changes**: Before submitting the pull request, thoroughly test your changes to ensure they work as expected and don't introduce any new issues.

o **Link to Relevant Issues**: If your pull request addresses an issue, make sure to reference the issue number in the description. This makes it easier for reviewers to understand why the changes were made. Example:

```bash

Fixes #45 - Add user authentication endpoint
```

2. **Best Practices for Reviewing Pull Requests**:

o **Review for Functionality and Code Quality**: When reviewing a pull request, ensure that the changes work as expected and adhere to the project's coding standards. Look for potential bugs, inefficiencies, or security concerns.

o **Be Constructive**: Provide feedback that is **constructive and clear**. If there's a problem with the code, suggest specific changes or improvements. Always be respectful and try to encourage a positive review process.

- o **Test the Changes**: If possible, check out the branch and run the code locally to ensure that the changes work as expected. Look for edge cases or scenarios where the code might fail.

- o **Check for Documentation**: Ensure that any new functionality is adequately documented, either in the code or in relevant project documentation.

- o **Focus on the Big Picture**: While reviewing the code, keep the overall project goals and best practices in mind. Ensure that the changes align with the project's objectives and direction.

Real-World Example: Managing Code Reviews and Incorporating Feedback

Let's walk through a real-world example of creating a pull request, receiving code review feedback, and incorporating that feedback into your pull request.

Scenario:

You're working on a **feature branch** called `feature/payment` to add a payment gateway to an e-commerce website. Once you've completed the work, you create a pull request to merge your changes into the `main` branch. Your teammates will review the code and provide feedback.

1. **Step 1: Create a Pull Request**:
   - You push your changes to the `feature/payment` branch and create a pull request to merge it into the `main` branch. In the description, you explain the changes:

     ```vbnet
     vbnet


     Title: Implemented Payment Gateway
     Integration

     Description: This PR integrates the
     payment gateway into the website. It
     includes:
     - Payment API integration
     - Frontend payment form for users
     - Basic error handling and validation

     Please review and provide feedback.
     ```

143

2. **Step 2: Code Review Feedback:**

   o One of your teammates, Sarah, reviews the pull request and leaves feedback:

     ▪ **Sarah**: "I noticed that the payment form lacks proper input validation. Can you add checks to ensure that the user enters a valid card number and expiration date?"

     ▪ **Sarah**: "Also, we're missing unit tests for the payment API integration. Can you write tests for the new code?"

3. **Step 3: Incorporate Feedback:**

   o You make the necessary changes based on Sarah's feedback:

     ▪ Add input validation for the card number and expiration date in the payment form.

     ▪ Write unit tests for the payment API integration.

   o After making these changes, you commit and push them to the same `feature/payment` branch:

```bash
git add payment.js tests/payment-tests.js
git commit -m "Added input validation and unit tests for payment API"
git push origin feature/payment
```

4. **Step 4: Update the Pull Request**:

   o Once you've pushed the changes, the pull request is automatically updated. Sarah will be notified that the changes have been made and that her feedback has been addressed.

5. **Step 5: Final Approval and Merge**:

   o After reviewing the updated pull request, Sarah approves the changes, and another teammate, John, merges the pull request into the `main` branch.

   o The new functionality is now part of the main project, and your changes are merged into the codebase.

Key Takeaways:

- **Pull requests** are a way to propose changes to a repository and allow for review and discussion before merging.

- **Creating a pull request** involves pushing your changes, providing a clear title and description, and selecting the target branch for merging.

- **Best practices for submitting pull requests** include keeping them small and focused, testing changes, and providing a clear explanation of the changes.

- **Code reviews** are essential for maintaining high-quality code. When reviewing, ensure the changes work as expected, adhere to code standards, and don't introduce bugs.

- **Incorporating feedback** from a code review involves making the necessary changes, committing them, and updating the pull request accordingly.

In the next chapter, we will discuss **Git workflows** and explore different strategies for managing branches and collaborating on projects in teams.

CHAPTER 13

MANAGING CONFLICTS

Merge conflicts are an inevitable part of working with Git, especially when collaborating on a project with multiple developers. A **merge conflict** occurs when Git cannot automatically reconcile differences between two branches that are being merged. This chapter will guide you through how to handle **merge conflicts effectively**, discuss strategies for resolving conflicts in **complex projects**, and provide a **real-world example** of how multiple team members can collaborate on the same codebase without causing issues.

How to Handle Merge Conflicts Effectively

Merge conflicts typically arise when two or more people make changes to the same line of code or the same file, and Git is unable to merge the changes automatically. Fortunately, Git provides the tools necessary to handle these situations, but it requires a manual process to resolve them.

Steps to Handle Merge Conflicts:

1. **Attempt to Merge:**
    - When you run the `git merge` command to merge one branch into another, Git will attempt to automatically combine the changes. If Git detects conflicts, it will stop and notify you about the merge conflict.
    - Example:

    bash

    ```
    git merge feature/authentication
    ```

2. **Identify Conflicted Files:**
    - Git will mark the files with conflicts as **unmerged**. To see which files are conflicted, you can use the `git status` command:

    bash

    ```
    git status
    ```

    Example output:

    bash

```
On branch main
Your branch is ahead of 'origin/main'
by 1 commit.
You have unmerged paths.
  (fix   conflicts   and   run   "git
commit")

Unmerged paths:
  (use "git add <file>..." to mark
resolution)
  both modified:   checkout.js
```

3. **Open the Conflicted Files**:

   o   Open the conflicted file(s) in your text editor. Git
       will insert conflict markers into the file to
       highlight the conflicting sections:

       Example:

       ```
       javascript
       ```

       ```
       <<<<<<< HEAD
       const        checkoutForm        =
       document.getElementById('checkout-
       form');
       =======
       ```

```
const          checkoutForm          =
document.querySelector('#checkout-
form');
>>>>>>> feature/authentication
```

- **HEAD** represents the changes in your current branch (the one you are merging into).

- The section between ======= and >>>>>> represents the changes in the branch you are merging from.

4. **Resolve the Conflict**:

   o Manually edit the file to choose which changes you want to keep. You can either:

   - Accept the changes from your current branch (HEAD).

   - Accept the changes from the branch being merged.

   - Combine both changes, if necessary.

After resolving the conflict, remove the conflict markers (<<<<<<<, =======, >>>>>>>).

5. **Stage the Resolved Files**:

150

o   Once the conflicts are resolved, stage the file(s) to mark them as resolved:

```bash
git add checkout.js
```

6. **Commit the Merge:**

    o   After staging the resolved files, commit the merge:

```bash
git commit -m "Resolved merge conflict in checkout.js"
```

If you were in the middle of a rebase, you would use `git rebase --continue` to proceed after resolving conflicts.

Strategies for Resolving Conflicts in Complex Projects

In larger projects, with many developers working on the same codebase, conflicts are more likely to occur. Here are some strategies to help manage and resolve conflicts effectively in **complex projects**:

1. **Frequent Pulls and Pushes**:
   o Regularly **pull changes** from the main branch into your feature branches to ensure that you are working with the most up-to-date version of the code. This reduces the likelihood of conflicts when you finally merge.

   o Similarly, **push your changes frequently** to the remote repository so that other developers can see your progress and avoid working on outdated code.

2. **Small, Focused Pull Requests**:
   o Keep your pull requests **small and focused** on a single change or feature. Large, monolithic pull requests that touch many parts of the codebase are more prone to conflicts.

   o Smaller pull requests are easier for reviewers to manage and can be merged more quickly, minimizing the time other developers will have to work with conflicting code.

3. **Clear Communication**:

- ○ **Communicate with your team** about which areas of the code you are working on. This can help avoid conflicts in the first place.

- ○ For example, if two developers are working on the same feature or file, they should coordinate their efforts to avoid conflicts.

4. **Use Git Rebase Instead of Merge**:

- ○ In some cases, using `git rebase` instead of `git merge` can help keep your commit history cleaner. Rebasing replays your changes on top of the latest commit from the base branch, ensuring that your changes are applied to the most recent version of the code.

- ○ Rebasing reduces merge commits and often leads to a cleaner history, though it requires more care in resolving conflicts during the rebase process.

5. **Use Visual Merge Tools**:

- ○ Git allows you to use **visual merge tools** to help resolve conflicts. Tools like **KDiff3**, **Meld**, or **P4Merge** can provide a graphical interface to make conflict resolution easier, especially when working with large files or complex changes.

o   To use a visual merge tool, run:

```bash
git mergetool
```

Real-World Example: Collaborating with Multiple Team Members on the Same Code

Let's go through a real-world example where multiple team members are working on the same code, and you need to manage merge conflicts during the process.

Scenario:

You and your team are building a collaborative web application. Your task is to implement a **user profile** page. Meanwhile, two other team members are working on features related to **user authentication** and **payment integration**, which also involve modifying the user.js file.

1. **Step 1: Initial Work and Conflict**:

    o   You start by working on the user profile page and modifying user.js to handle displaying user information.

o   At the same time, your colleague Sarah is working on integrating the authentication logic into `user.js`. Both of you make changes to the same lines of code, and when Sarah pushes her changes to the remote repository, Git alerts her to a merge conflict.

2. **Step 2: Attempt to Merge**:

o   You run the following command to merge Sarah's changes into your branch:

```bash
git merge feature/authentication
```

o   Git detects the conflict in `user.js` and stops the merge process.

3. **Step 3: Identify and Resolve the Conflict**:

o   You run `git status` to see the conflicted file:

```bash
git status
```

o   Git shows `user.js` as the conflicted file, and you open it to resolve the conflict.

4. **Step 4: Manual Conflict Resolution**:

   o In `user.js`, Git shows that both you and Sarah modified the same lines of code. You discuss the conflict with Sarah and decide on how to combine both changes.

   o After making the necessary adjustments and removing the conflict markers, you stage the resolved file:

   ```bash
   git add user.js
   ```

5. **Step 5: Finalize the Merge**:

   o Once the conflict is resolved, you commit the merge:

   ```bash
   git commit -m "Resolved merge conflict in user.js"
   ```

6. **Step 6: Push Changes**:

   o You push the merged changes to the remote repository:

```
bash
```

```
git push origin feature/profile
```

7. **Step 7: Review and Integration**:

   o   Finally, you create a pull request to merge the `feature/profile` branch into the `main` branch. After reviewing the changes, your team approves the pull request, and the feature is integrated into the main project.

Key Takeaways:

- **Merge conflicts** occur when Git cannot automatically merge changes from two branches. They are common in collaborative projects, especially when multiple developers work on the same files.

- To handle conflicts, manually resolve the conflicting sections of code, stage the resolved files, and commit the changes.

- **Best practices** for avoiding and resolving conflicts include frequent pulls, small pull requests, clear communication with team members, and using tools like **rebase** and **visual merge tools**.

- In complex projects with multiple team members, it's important to coordinate work and follow strategies to reduce the chances of conflicts while maintaining a clean Git history.

In the next chapter, we will explore **advanced Git workflows** and best practices for managing large projects and teams efficiently.

CHAPTER 14

GIT HOOKS: AUTOMATING TASKS

Git hooks are powerful tools that allow you to automate tasks and enforce workflows at various points in your Git process. These hooks enable you to run scripts at specific moments in your development cycle—such as before a commit is made, before pushing changes to a remote repository, or after a commit is completed. By leveraging Git hooks, you can ensure that certain tasks (like running tests, checking code style, or automating deployments) are executed automatically, making your development process more efficient and less error-prone.

In this chapter, we'll explore **what Git hooks are**, how to set up **pre-commit**, **pre-push**, and **post-commit hooks**, and walk through a **real-world example** of running tests automatically before committing your code.

What Are Git Hooks and How Can They Help Automate Workflows?

Git hooks are scripts that Git automatically executes at certain points in the Git workflow. These hooks can help automate repetitive tasks, such as:

- Running tests before committing code.
- Ensuring code style consistency.
- Validating commit messages.
- Deploying code after a successful commit.

Git hooks are stored in the `.git/hooks` directory of a repository, and they are triggered by specific Git actions. For example, you can set up a **pre-commit hook** to run unit tests before allowing a commit, or a **post-commit hook** to send a notification once the commit has been made.

Some common Git hooks include:

- **pre-commit**: Runs before a commit is made, useful for tasks like linting and testing.

- **pre-push**: Runs before code is pushed to a remote repository, useful for checking whether everything is ready for sharing with others.

- **post-commit**: Runs after a commit is completed, useful for running automated tasks like notifications or deployments.

Setting Up Pre-commit, Pre-push, and Post-commit Hooks

1. **Locating the Hooks Directory**:

    o Git hooks are located in the `.git/hooks` directory of your project. Each hook has its own script file, and Git provides sample files (with `.sample` extensions) for each type of hook.

    o To find the hooks directory, navigate to the root of your Git repository and look inside the `.git/hooks` folder:

    bash

    ```
    cd .git/hooks
    ```

2. **Making Hooks Executable**:

- o The hook scripts are usually provided as sample files with `.sample` extensions. To use a hook, you need to remove the `.sample` extension and make the file executable.

- o For example, to set up the `pre-commit` hook, rename the sample file:

bash

```
mv pre-commit.sample pre-commit
chmod +x pre-commit
```

3. **Configuring Pre-commit Hooks**:

- o The `pre-commit` hook runs before a commit is made. It's useful for running automated tasks like linting, formatting, or testing code.

Example: Running Tests Before Committing:

- o Suppose you want to run unit tests automatically every time you make a commit to ensure that your code is stable. In the `pre-commit` hook, you could add a script to run the tests:

bash

162

```
#! /bin/sh
# Run tests before commit
npm test
if [ $? -ne 0 ]; then
    echo   "Tests   failed!   Commit
aborted."
    exit 1
fi
```

o   This script runs the `npm test` command before each commit. If the tests fail (i.e., the exit status is not 0), the commit is aborted.

4. **Setting Up Pre-push Hooks**:

o   The `pre-push` hook runs before you push code to a remote repository. It's useful for checking that everything is in order before sharing your code with others.

Example: Running Linting Before Pushing:

o   You could set up a `pre-push` hook to run a linting tool like ESLint to ensure that the code follows coding standards:

```
bash
```

163

```
#! /bin/sh
# Run linting before push
npm run lint
if [ $? -ne 0 ]; then
   echo    "Linting    failed!    Push
aborted."
   exit 1
fi
```

o   This script will run `npm run lint` before every push. If the linting fails, the push is aborted, ensuring that only well-formatted code is pushed to the remote repository.

5.   **Setting Up Post-commit Hooks**:

o   The `post-commit` hook runs after a commit is made, which can be useful for tasks like sending notifications, updating a documentation system, or triggering a deployment.

Example: Sending a Notification After Commit:

o   You can configure a `post-commit` hook to send an email or Slack notification each time a commit is made:

```
bash
```

```
#! /bin/sh
# Send notification after commit
echo "A new commit has been made!" |
mail -s "Git Commit Notification"
your_email@example.com
```

   o   This script sends an email after each commit, notifying you (or your team) that a new commit has been made.

Real-World Example: Running Tests Before Committing Code

Let's explore a **real-world example** where we use Git hooks to ensure that unit tests are run before committing code, ensuring that no broken code is committed.

Scenario:

You're working on a collaborative project where stability is crucial. Your team has a set of unit tests in place, and you want to prevent committing code that doesn't pass these tests. You can use a `pre-commit` hook to run the tests automatically before any code is committed.

1. **Step 1: Create the Pre-commit Hook**:

o Navigate to the .git/hooks directory and create or edit the pre-commit hook:

```
bash

cd .git/hooks
touch pre-commit
```

2. **Step 2: Add the Test Script:**

o Open the pre-commit file in your text editor and add the following script:

```
bash

#! /bin/sh
# Run tests before commit
npm test
if [ $? -ne 0 ]; then
    echo    "Tests    failed!    Commit
aborted."
    exit 1
fi
```

o This script runs npm test, and if any test fails (non-zero exit status), it aborts the commit process.

3. **Step 3: Make the Hook Executable:**

166

o   Make sure the hook is executable by running:

```bash
```

```
chmod +x pre-commit
```

4. **Step 4: Commit Changes**:

o   Now, whenever you try to commit changes, Git will run the tests first. If the tests pass, the commit proceeds. If they fail, the commit is aborted.

o   Example:

```bash
```

```
git commit -m "Added new feature"
```

If the tests fail, the commit will be stopped, and the message "Tests failed! Commit aborted." will be displayed.

5. **Step 5: Push Changes**:

o   If your tests pass and you commit the changes, you can then push the changes to the remote repository using:

```bash
```

```
git push origin feature/your-feature
```

Key Takeaways:

- **Git hooks** are scripts that allow you to automate tasks at various points in the Git workflow. They can help enforce workflows, such as running tests, linting code, or sending notifications.

- **Pre-commit hooks** run before a commit and are commonly used for tasks like testing, linting, or formatting code.

- **Pre-push hooks** run before pushing code to the remote repository, ensuring that code is properly validated before sharing it with others.

- **Post-commit hooks** run after a commit is made and are useful for tasks like notifications or triggering further actions.

- Using Git hooks ensures that important tasks, like testing or formatting, are automatically handled, reducing the chance of errors and improving your development workflow.

In the next chapter, we will dive deeper into **Git workflows**, focusing on popular strategies for managing branches and collaborations in large projects.

CHAPTER 15

GIT SUBMODULES: MANAGING DEPENDENCIES

When managing a large codebase, you often find that some components of your project are developed and maintained separately. In such cases, it can be useful to incorporate external repositories or libraries into your project without duplicating the code. **Git submodules** provide a way to do this. They allow you to include one Git repository as a subdirectory of another Git repository, enabling you to manage dependencies more efficiently.

In this chapter, we'll explore **what Git submodules are**, **when to use them**, and how to **add and update submodules** in your project. We will also go through a **real-world example** of managing external libraries as submodules, which is a common use case for Git submodules.

What Are Git Submodules and When Should You Use Them?

A **Git submodule** is essentially a Git repository embedded inside another Git repository. It allows you to include an external project or library into your repository as a subdirectory, while still keeping the external project in its own repository.

Git submodules are useful when you want to:

- **Incorporate external libraries** or dependencies into your project without merging the code into your main repository.
- **Track a specific version** of an external repository and keep it up to date with the latest changes.
- **Maintain separate development processes**: If you're working on multiple projects that share certain dependencies or libraries, you can treat each dependency as its own separate repository and use Git submodules to manage them.

Use Cases for Git Submodules:

1. **Managing external libraries**: When you use a third-party library that has its own development process and

repository, you can include it as a submodule to ensure you're working with a specific version of the library.

2. **Shared dependencies**: When multiple projects share a common codebase or library, using submodules allows you to reuse the same codebase across different projects.

3. **Component-based development**: When developing large software systems that consist of multiple components, each with its own repository, submodules allow you to organize and manage these components efficiently.

Adding and Updating Submodules in Your Project

To work with submodules in Git, you'll need to know how to add and update them. Here are the steps to add a submodule to your repository and keep it up to date.

1. **Adding a Submodule**:

   o To add a submodule, use the `git submodule add` command followed by the URL of the external repository and the directory where you want the submodule to reside in your project.

   Example:

```
bash
```

```
git          submodule          add
https://github.com/username/external-
library.git path/to/submodule-directory
```

This will:

- o Clone the external repository into the specified directory (`path/to/submodule-directory`).
- o Create a `.gitmodules` file that contains metadata about the submodule, including its URL and path.
- o Stage the changes (i.e., the addition of the submodule) in your repository.

After adding the submodule, you need to commit the changes:

```
bash
```

```
git commit -m "Added submodule external-
library"
```

2. **Cloning a Repository with Submodules:**

o If you're cloning a repository that already contains submodules, you'll need to initialize and update the submodules after cloning:

bash

```
git    clone    https://github.com/your-
username/your-repo.git
cd your-repo
git submodule update --init --recursive
```

The --recursive option ensures that all submodules and any nested submodules are cloned and initialized.

3. **Updating Submodules**:

o If the external submodule repository has new changes, you can update it to the latest commit using the git submodule update command:

bash

```
git    submodule    update    --remote
path/to/submodule-directory
```

This fetches the latest changes from the submodule repository and updates the submodule in your project to the latest commit from the submodule's default branch.

Alternatively, you can also navigate to the submodule directory and run a standard Git pull:

```bash
cd path/to/submodule-directory
git pull origin master
```

4. **Removing a Submodule**:

    o   If you no longer need a submodule in your project, you can remove it by following these steps:

        1. Remove the submodule entry from .gitmodules:

        ```bash
        git submodule deinit path/to/submodule-directory
        git rm path/to/submodule-directory
        ```

        2. Commit the changes:

        ```bash
        ```

175

```
git    commit    -m    "Removed
submodule external-library"
```

3. Clean up any remaining submodule files:

```bash
rm                              -rf
.git/modules/path/to/submodul
e-directory
```

Real-World Example: Managing External Libraries as Submodules

Let's walk through a real-world example of using Git submodules to manage an external library.

Scenario:

You're building a web application, and you want to use a third-party JavaScript library for managing forms (e.g., `formLib`). Instead of ing the entire library's code into your project, you decide to include it as a submodule, allowing you to easily update it whenever the library's repository is updated.

1. **Step 1: Add the Submodule**:

- o First, navigate to your project directory and add the external library as a submodule:

  ```bash
  ```

  ```
  git          submodule          add
  https://github.com/example/formLib.
  git external/formLib
  ```

- o This adds the external library into the external/formLib directory and stages the changes in your repository.

2. **Step 2: Commit the Submodule**:

   - o After adding the submodule, commit the changes:

     ```bash
     ```

     ```
     git commit -m "Added formLib as a
     submodule"
     ```

3. **Step 3: Using the Submodule in Your Project**:

   - o Now, you can use the library in your project as if it were part of the main repository. For example, in your index.js file:

```javascript
import formLib from
'./external/formLib';
formLib.initialize();
```

4. **Step 4: Updating the Submodule**:

   o Periodically, you'll want to check if the external library has been updated. You can update the submodule by navigating to the submodule directory and pulling the latest changes:

   ```bash
   cd external/formLib
   git pull origin master
   ```

   o Alternatively, you can update all submodules in one go:

   ```bash
   git submodule update --remote
   ```

5. **Step 5: Commit the Update**:

   o After updating the submodule, commit the updated reference in your main repository:

178

```
bash
```

```
git    commit   -m   "Updated   formLib
submodule to latest version"
```

6. **Step 6: Pushing the Changes**:

   o Finally, push the changes to the remote repository:

```
bash
```

```
git push origin main
```

Key Takeaways:

- **Git submodules** are a way to include an external repository as a subdirectory in your project, allowing you to manage dependencies or shared components in a clean and organized way.

- To **add a submodule**, use `git submodule add <repository_url> <path>`.

- **Updating submodules** can be done with `git submodule update --remote`.

- Submodules are useful for managing external libraries or code that you want to include in your project while keeping it in its own repository.

- You can also **remove submodules** by deinitializing and removing the corresponding entries in `.gitmodules` and the repository.

In the next chapter, we'll explore **Git workflows** in more detail, including strategies for managing branching, merging, and collaboration in large, complex projects.

CHAPTER 16

USING GIT WITH CONTINUOUS INTEGRATION/CONTINUOUS DEPLOYMENT (CI/CD)

Integrating **Git** with **Continuous Integration (CI)** and **Continuous Deployment (CD)** tools is a powerful way to automate the development workflow. By combining Git with CI/CD tools like **Jenkins, Travis CI, or GitHub Actions**, you can streamline processes such as **automated testing, deployment,** and **code quality checks.** This chapter will explore how to integrate Git with these tools, automate key tasks, and walk through a **real-world example** of setting up automated deployments for a web application.

Integrating Git with CI/CD Tools like Jenkins, Travis CI, or GitHub Actions

Continuous Integration (CI) is the practice of automatically testing and integrating changes into a shared repository multiple times per day. This helps catch errors early and ensures that the codebase remains in a deployable state.

Continuous Deployment (CD) goes a step further by automatically deploying changes to a production or staging environment after passing tests and integration steps, removing the need for manual intervention.

Git works seamlessly with CI/CD tools to automate various parts of the development pipeline. Below, we'll explore how to integrate Git with three popular CI/CD tools: **Jenkins**, **Travis CI**, and **GitHub Actions**.

1. Integrating Git with Jenkins

Jenkins is an open-source automation server that supports CI/CD pipelines. It is highly customizable and has a wide range of plugins for integration with Git and other tools.

Setting up Jenkins with Git:

1. **Install Jenkins**:
   o You can install Jenkins by following the official documentation for your operating system. After

installation, start Jenkins and navigate to its web interface (typically `http://localhost:8080`).

2. **Install the Git Plugin**:

   o Jenkins requires the Git plugin to integrate with Git repositories. You can install the plugin by going to **Manage Jenkins** > **Manage Plugins** and searching for **Git Plugin**.

3. **Create a New Jenkins Job**:

   o In Jenkins, create a new job by selecting **New Item**.

   o Choose the type of project (usually **Freestyle Project**) and enter a name.

4. **Configure Git Repository**:

   o Under the **Source Code Management** section, select **Git** and enter the repository URL (e.g., `https://github.com/username/repository-name.git`).

   o If your repository is private, you'll need to provide credentials (such as SSH keys or username/password).

5. **Set Build Triggers**:

- o Set a trigger to tell Jenkins when to build your project. For example, you can choose to trigger a build every time there's a **push** to the repository or at scheduled intervals.

- o To trigger a build on each push to GitHub, you can enable **GitHub hook trigger for GITScm polling**.

6. **Define Build Steps**:

- o In the **Build** section, you can add steps to run tests, build the application, or deploy it. For example, you could run a test suite:

```bash

npm install
npm test
```

7. **Post-build Actions**:

- o You can also set up **post-build actions** like sending email notifications or deploying your application to a server or cloud platform.

8. **Start the Jenkins Job**:

- o Save your job and trigger a build. Jenkins will automatically pull the latest code from your Git

184

repository, run the tests, and execute other steps you have defined.

---

2. Integrating Git with Travis CI

Travis CI is a cloud-based CI service that integrates directly with GitHub repositories. It provides an easy way to set up automated testing and deployment pipelines.

Setting up Travis CI with GitHub:

1. **Link Your GitHub Repository to Travis CI:**
   - Sign up for a Travis CI account using your GitHub account (https://travis-ci.org/).
   - After signing in, enable your repository in the Travis CI dashboard.

2. **Create a `.travis.yml` File:**
   - In your GitHub repository, create a `.travis.yml` file at the root of the project. This YAML file defines the build pipeline and specifies tasks to run.

Example `.travis.yml` for a Node.js project:

```yaml
language: node_js
node_js:
  - "14"

script:
  - npm install
  - npm test
```

This configuration tells Travis CI to:

- o   Use **Node.js version 14**.

- o   Run `npm install` to install dependencies.

- o   Run `npm test` to execute tests.

3. **Push to GitHub**:

- o   After committing the `.travis.yml` file to your Git repository, push the changes to GitHub. Travis CI will automatically detect the push and trigger a build.

4. **View Build Results**:

- o   You can view the build results on the Travis CI dashboard. If the tests pass, the build is successful.

186

If there's an issue, you'll see detailed logs and can troubleshoot the failure.

3. Integrating Git with GitHub Actions

GitHub Actions is GitHub's own CI/CD tool, which allows you to automate workflows directly within GitHub repositories. It's tightly integrated with GitHub and is a great choice for GitHub-based projects.

Setting up GitHub Actions with Your Repository:

1. **Create a Workflow File:**
   o In your GitHub repository, create a directory called `.github/workflows` and add a YAML file for your workflow. For example, create a file called `ci.yml` in `.github/workflows/`.

   Example `ci.yml` for a Node.js project:

```yaml
name: CI Workflow
```

187

```
on:
  push:
    branches:
      - main
  pull_request:
    branches:
      - main

jobs:
  test:
    runs-on: ubuntu-latest

    steps:
      - name: Checkout code
        uses: actions/checkout@v2

      - name: Set up Node.js
        uses: actions/setup-node@v2
        with:
          node-version: '14'

      - name: Install dependencies
        run: npm install

      - name: Run tests
        run: npm test
```

This file configures GitHub Actions to:

o   Trigger on **push** and **pull request** events to the `main` branch.

o   Set up **Node.js** version 14.

o   Install dependencies and run tests using `npm`.

2. **Commit and Push the Workflow**:

o   Commit the `.github/workflows/ci.yml` file to your GitHub repository and push the changes.

3. **Automatic Execution**:

o   GitHub Actions will automatically trigger the workflow whenever there is a push or pull request to the `main` branch. You can view the progress and results in the **Actions** tab of your GitHub repository.

Automating Testing, Deployment, and Code Quality Checks Using Git

With Git and CI/CD tools, you can automate a wide range of tasks, including:

1. **Automated Testing**:

- o   Running unit tests, integration tests, or end-to-end tests on each push or pull request.

- o   Ensuring that your code is thoroughly tested before merging or deploying it.

2. **Automated Deployment**:

- o   Automatically deploying your code to staging or production environments once the tests pass.

- o   This can include deploying to cloud platforms like **AWS**, **Azure**, or **Heroku**, or to on-premise servers.

3. **Code Quality Checks**:

- o   Running **linters** and **formatters** to ensure that the code adheres to style guides and best practices.

- o   You can also use tools like **SonarQube** to run static analysis on your code and check for vulnerabilities.

Example: Adding a linter to a GitHub Actions workflow:

yaml

```
- name: Run linter
  run: npm run lint
```

Real-World Example: Setting Up Automated Deployments for a Web Application

Let's walk through a real-world example of setting up **automated deployments** for a web application using **GitHub Actions**.

Scenario:

You are working on a Node.js web application, and you want to automatically deploy it to **Heroku** every time code is pushed to the `main` branch.

1. **Step 1: Set Up Heroku**:
   o Create a Heroku application if you haven't already by following the instructions on the Heroku dashboard.

2. **Step 2: Generate Heroku API Key**:
   o To allow GitHub Actions to deploy to Heroku, generate an API key from your Heroku account settings.

3. **Step 3: Create the GitHub Actions Workflow**:
   o In your GitHub repository, create the `.github/workflows/deploy.yml` file:

191

```yaml
yaml

name: Deploy to Heroku

on:
  push:
    branches:
      - main

jobs:
  deploy:
    runs-on: ubuntu-latest

    steps:
      - name: Checkout code
        uses: actions/checkout@v2

      - name: Set up Node.js
        uses: actions/setup-node@v2
        with:
          node-version: '14'

      - name: Install dependencies
        run: npm install

      - name: Log in to Heroku
        run: |
          echo          "HEROKU_API_KEY=${{
secrets.HEROKU_API_KEY }}" > $GITHUB_ENV
```

```
        curl            https://cli-
assets.heroku.com/install.sh | sh
        heroku login -i


    - name: Deploy to Heroku
      run: |
        git     remote     add     heroku
https://git.heroku.com/your-app-name.git
        git push heroku main
```

- o This workflow will:

  - Trigger on every push to the `main` branch.

  - Set up Node.js, install dependencies, and deploy the code to Heroku.

4. **Step 4: Set Secrets in GitHub**:

   - o Add your Heroku API key as a secret in the GitHub repository's settings:

     - Go to **Settings** > **Secrets** and add a new secret named `HEROKU_API_KEY`.

5. **Step 5: Commit and Push the Workflow**:

   - o Commit the workflow file and push it to GitHub. Now, every time you push code to `main`, GitHub Actions will automatically deploy your application to Heroku.

Key Takeaways:

- **CI/CD** tools like Jenkins, Travis CI, and GitHub Actions can automate testing, deployment, and other tasks in your Git workflow.

- **GitHub Actions** integrates directly with GitHub repositories and is an excellent tool for automating workflows.

- **Automated testing** ensures that your code is thoroughly tested before being merged.

- **Automated deployment** helps you deploy your application to staging or production environments without manual intervention, streamlining the release process.

- By setting up **automated workflows**, you can ensure high-quality code and faster delivery.

In the next chapter, we'll explore **advanced Git workflows**, including strategies for managing releases, working with multiple environments, and handling large-scale projects.

CHAPTER 17

GIT PERFORMANCE OPTIMIZATION

As projects grow in size and complexity, Git can face performance challenges, particularly when dealing with **large repositories** and **many contributors**. Large-scale codebases with numerous files and commit histories can make basic Git operations (like cloning, fetching, and checking out branches) slow and cumbersome. In this chapter, we'll explore how to handle large repositories efficiently, optimize Git operations for speed and performance, and provide a **real-world example** of managing a large-scale codebase with efficient Git workflows.

How to Handle Large Repositories Efficiently

Git is designed to handle large codebases, but the performance of basic Git operations can degrade as the repository grows. To keep things running smoothly, there are several strategies you can implement to improve Git's performance when working with large repositories.

195

1. **Use Shallow Clones**:

   o **Shallow clones** only download a specific number of commits from the repository's history, which can drastically reduce the size of the repository on your local machine. This is particularly useful when you only need the latest state of the project and don't need the entire commit history.

   Example:

   ```bash
   git clone --depth 1 https://github.com/username/repository.git
   ```

   This will clone the repository, but only the latest commit will be downloaded. You can later fetch more commits if needed using:

   ```bash
   git fetch --depth=50
   ```

2. **Use Sparse Checkout**:

○ **Sparse checkout** allows you to check out only a subset of the files in a repository, which can be helpful if you only need to work with specific directories or files.

Steps to enable sparse checkout:

○ First, enable the feature:

```bash
```

```
git config core.sparseCheckout true
```

○ Then, define the directories/files you want to check out by adding them to the `.git/info/sparse-checkout` file. For example, if you only want to work on files in the `src/` directory:

```bash
```

```
echo "src/*" >> .git/info/sparse-
checkout
```

○ Finally, run:

```bash
```

197

```
git checkout main
```

This will only check out files in the `src/` directory, making the repository more manageable.

3. **Split Large Repositories (Monorepo):**

   o If your repository has grown too large, it may be beneficial to split it into multiple smaller repositories (also known as a **monorepo**). This is especially useful if different parts of the project are only loosely coupled or can be worked on independently.

   o Git doesn't natively support splitting large repositories, but there are third-party tools like **git-submodules** and **git-filter-repo** that can help you break a monolithic repository into smaller, more manageable ones.

4. **Use Git LFS (Large File Storage):**

   o For repositories that include large binary files (such as images, videos, or data files), Git LFS (Large File Storage) is a specialized Git extension

198

that stores large files outside the Git repository and replaces them with small pointers.

Steps to use Git LFS:

o   Install Git LFS:

```bash
git lfs install
```

o   Track large files:

```bash
git lfs track "*.jpg"
```

o   Add, commit, and push the large files as usual. Git LFS will handle storing them externally.

5. **Avoid Large Commits and Large Histories**:

o   Avoid committing a large number of files or very large files in a single commit. Break down large changes into smaller, more manageable commits.

o   If the repository has an excessively long history, consider cleaning up old, irrelevant branches and commits that are no longer needed.

Optimizing Git Operations for Speed and Performance

There are several techniques you can apply to optimize the speed and efficiency of Git operations, especially when dealing with large repositories or a complex project history.

1. **Optimize Git Configuration**:

   o Some Git configurations can improve performance. For example, setting `core.preloadIndex` to `true` can improve performance during `git status` checks:

   bash

   ```
   git        config        --global
   core.preloadIndex true
   ```

2. **Use Git's `git gc` (Garbage Collection)**:

   o Git maintains a repository's history by creating objects for every change. Over time, these objects can accumulate and slow down Git operations. Running `git gc` periodically will clean up unnecessary files and optimize the repository.

o Run the following command to initiate garbage collection:

```bash
```

```
git gc
```

o This will remove any unreachable objects and compress the repository's history to improve speed.

3. **Avoid Frequent `git status` Calls**:

o `git status` can be slow in large repositories because Git needs to check the entire working directory for changes. Avoid calling `git status` too frequently when working with large codebases.

4. **Optimize the `.gitignore` File**:

o Ensure your `.gitignore` file is configured properly to prevent unnecessary files from being tracked by Git. This will reduce the size of the repository and improve performance during operations like commits and checkouts.

5. **Use `git fsck` to Check Repository Integrity**:

o The `git fsck` command checks the integrity of the Git repository and ensures that everything is in order. Running this command periodically can help prevent performance issues:

```bash
git fsck --full
```

Real-World Example: Managing a Large-Scale Codebase with Efficient Git Workflows

Let's consider a **real-world scenario** where you're managing a **large-scale web application** repository that contains multiple components and dependencies. Your team has decided to split the project into multiple repositories, with each component stored in its own Git repository. You also use **Git LFS** to handle large media files and **Git submodules** for managing shared libraries.

1. **Step 1: Structuring the Project**:
   o You have a monorepo that includes the following components:
      ▪ **Web frontend** (React app)
      ▪ **Backend API** (Node.js app)

202

- **Shared libraries** (common utilities)

Each component is stored in its own Git repository to allow independent development.

2. **Step 2: Using Submodules for Shared Libraries**:

   o The **shared libraries** (e.g., `auth-lib`, `payment-lib`) are stored in separate Git repositories. These libraries are included in the main repository using **Git submodules** to keep track of their versions:

   bash

   ```
   git          submodule          add
   https://github.com/username/auth-
   lib.git libs/auth-lib
   ```

3. **Step 3: Optimizing with Git LFS**:

   o To manage large assets like images, videos, and other binary files, you configure **Git LFS** to handle these files:

   bash

   ```
   git lfs track "*.png"
   ```

203

```
git lfs track "*.mp4"
```

4. **Step 4: Implementing Sparse Checkout**:

   o Your frontend team only needs to work on the frontend directory. By enabling **sparse checkout**, you limit the files checked out on their machines, which saves bandwidth and improves Git performance:

   bash

   ```
   git config core.sparseCheckout true
   echo         "frontend/*"         >>
   .git/info/sparse-checkout
   git checkout main
   ```

5. **Step 5: Performance Tuning with Git Configurations**:

   o You optimize the Git configuration to enhance performance during common operations like git status and git commit. The team sets up the following configuration:

   bash

   ```
   git         config         --global
   core.preloadIndex true
   ```

```
git config --global core.quotepath
false
```

6. **Step 6: Running Periodic Garbage Collection**:

   o To keep the repository optimized and reduce its size over time, you schedule regular **garbage collection** using Git's `git gc` command:

   bash

   ```
   git gc --auto
   ```

7. **Step 7: Regular Submodule Updates**:

   o To update the submodules (e.g., `auth-lib`), the development team periodically runs:

   bash

   ```
   git submodule update --remote
   ```

Key Takeaways:

- **Git submodules** are useful for managing external libraries and dependencies within a project without duplicating code.

- **Shallow clones, sparse checkout**, and **Git LFS** help optimize large repositories by reducing their size and focusing on specific parts of the project.

- **Git configuration optimizations** like `core.preloadIndex` and `git gc` improve the performance of Git operations.

- Managing a **large-scale codebase** requires a combination of **Git submodules**, **Git LFS**, and **periodic maintenance** to ensure that Git operations remain fast and efficient.

In the next chapter, we'll dive into **Git security practices**, focusing on how to securely manage credentials, handle sensitive data, and protect your repository.

CHAPTER 18

REPOSITORY MAINTENANCE: PRUNING AND GARBAGE COLLECTION

As Git repositories grow and evolve, they can accumulate unnecessary files, old branches, and unreachable objects that can slow down performance and make the repository harder to manage. Regular **repository maintenance** is essential to keep the repository clean, organized, and performant. In this chapter, we'll discuss how to maintain a Git repository effectively using commands like `git gc` (garbage collection) and `git prune`, and provide a **real-world example** of cleaning up old branches and commits to maintain repository health.

Keeping Repositories Clean and Organized

A healthy Git repository is one that is free of unnecessary files, obsolete branches, and large, unused objects. As developers work on a project, several factors can contribute to a bloated and disorganized repository:

- **Unmerged branches**: Feature branches, bug-fix branches, and other temporary branches that are no longer needed after being merged.

- **Old commits**: Commits that have been superseded by newer changes, especially when working on experimental features or rebasing.

- **Orphaned objects**: Objects in the repository that are no longer referenced by any commits (e.g., leftover files, blobs, or commits from deleted branches).

Without regular maintenance, these unnecessary files and objects can accumulate, slowing down operations like cloning, fetching, and checking out branches. To maintain the health of a repository, it's important to periodically clean it up.

Using `git gc` and `git prune` for Maintenance

Git provides two powerful tools for cleaning up repositories: **git gc (garbage collection)** and **git prune**. Let's explore each tool and its purpose in maintaining a Git repository.

1. **`git gc` (Garbage Collection)**:

    o **`git gc`** is a command used to optimize the repository by cleaning up unnecessary files and compressing the repository's history to improve performance. It performs several maintenance tasks, such as:

    - Removing unreachable objects (objects that are no longer referenced by any branch or commit).

    - Compressing file history into a more efficient form to save space and improve speed.

    - Repacking loose objects (individual objects that are stored separately) into a single pack file.

    How to Run `git gc`:

    o To perform garbage collection, simply run:

    ```bash
    ```

    ```
    git gc
    ```

    o By default, this command will:

- Remove unreachable objects.
- Compress objects and store them efficiently.
- Optimize the repository to improve overall performance.

Automatic Garbage Collection:

o Git runs garbage collection automatically in the background at certain times, such as during operations like `git commit` or `git push`. However, you can manually trigger `git gc` to ensure your repository is optimized after significant changes, such as after a large merge or rebase.

o You can also set up Git to automatically run garbage collection in the background after a certain number of commits:

```bash
git config --global gc.auto 100
```

This configuration will automatically trigger garbage collection after 100 commits.

210

2. `git prune`:

    o **git prune** is a command used to remove **unreachable objects** from the repository. Unreachable objects are commits or files that are no longer referenced by any branch or tag.

    o While `git gc` removes unreachable objects as part of its operations, you can use `git prune` for more aggressive pruning, especially in large repositories that have a lot of abandoned branches or commits.

How to Run `git prune`:

    o To prune unreachable objects, run:

```bash
git prune
```

Caution: Unlike `git gc`, which is generally safe to run, `git prune` permanently deletes unreachable objects. You should use it with care and ensure that no important data is lost.

o You can run `git prune` on its own or in conjunction with `git gc` to ensure your repository is fully cleaned up.

Real-World Example: Cleaning Up Old Branches and Commits to Maintain Repository Health

Let's walk through a **real-world example** of cleaning up old branches and commits to maintain the health of a large-scale Git repository.

Scenario:

You are working on a collaborative web development project, and over time, numerous feature branches have been created, worked on, and merged. Some of these branches are still present in the repository, even though they have already been merged into the `main` branch. Additionally, the repository has accumulated many unreachable objects from old commits that are no longer part of the project's history.

1. **Step 1: Delete Merged Feature Branches**:

- o After a feature branch is merged into `main`, it is no longer needed and can be safely deleted. To identify merged branches:

```bash
git branch --merged main
```

- o This will list all the branches that have been merged into the `main` branch. You can then delete these branches:

```bash
git branch -d feature/old-feature-branch
```

- o If you want to delete remote branches as well, use:

```bash
git push origin --delete feature/old-feature-branch
```

2. **Step 2: Perform Garbage Collection:**

o   After cleaning up merged branches, it's a good idea to run **git gc** to clean up any unnecessary objects in the repository:

```
bash
```

```
git gc
```

o   This will remove unreachable objects, compress the repository history, and optimize the repository for better performance.

3. **Step 3: Prune Unreachable Objects**:

o   After garbage collection, you may still have unreachable objects that were created by abandoned commits, branches, or other operations. Run **git prune** to remove these objects:

```
bash
```

```
git prune
```

o   This will permanently delete any objects that are no longer reachable from any branch or commit.

4. **Step 4: Verify Repository Health**:

○ After running `git gc` and `git prune`, you can verify the health of the repository using the `git fsck` (file system check) command:

```bash
```

```
git fsck
```

○ This command checks the integrity of the repository and ensures that all objects are properly referenced.

5. **Step 5: Periodic Cleanup:**

○ To keep your repository healthy over time, it's a good practice to periodically perform cleanup tasks like `git gc` and `git prune`, especially after major merges or rebases. You can schedule these tasks to run automatically in your repository's maintenance process.

Key Takeaways:

• **Repository maintenance** is essential for keeping large Git repositories clean, organized, and efficient. Over time, repositories can accumulate old branches, unnecessary objects, and bloat, which can slow down operations.

- **git gc (garbage collection)** optimizes the repository by removing unreachable objects and compressing the repository's history.

- **git prune** is an advanced command that permanently deletes unreachable objects and is useful for cleaning up old commits and data that are no longer part of the repository's history.

- Regularly cleaning up old branches and commits is important to **maintain repository health**, improve performance, and reduce storage requirements.

In the next chapter, we will explore **advanced Git workflows** for large teams and projects, focusing on strategies for managing feature branches, releases, and collaborative development.

CHAPTER 19

GIT IN A TEAM ENVIRONMENT

In professional development, Git is an essential tool for collaboration, allowing multiple developers to work on the same project simultaneously. However, to ensure smooth collaboration and maintain high-quality code, it's crucial to follow best practices and adopt efficient Git workflows. In this chapter, we'll cover **best practices** for using Git in team projects, explore various **workflow models** like **Git Flow**, **GitHub Flow**, and **GitLab Flow**, and walk through a **real-world example** of managing multiple developers on a project using a well-defined Git workflow.

Best Practices for Using Git in Team Projects

1. **Frequent and Meaningful Commits**:
   o   Developers should commit their changes frequently, ideally after completing small, logical units of work. Frequent commits make it easier to track progress, revert changes if necessary, and collaborate with others.

o Each commit should include a **meaningful message** that clearly explains the change. A good commit message provides context for the change and helps collaborators understand the purpose of the commit.

2. **Pull Changes Frequently**:

   o Developers should pull changes from the main branch (`main` or `develop`) regularly to stay up-to-date with the latest code from their teammates. This helps avoid **merge conflicts** and ensures everyone is working on the most recent version of the project.

   o Using `git pull --rebase` is recommended in many workflows to ensure a linear commit history, which reduces merge commits.

3. **Work in Feature Branches**:

   o Always work in **feature branches** instead of committing directly to the `main` branch. Feature branches allow developers to isolate their work and keep the `main` branch stable.

   o Feature branches should be short-lived and focused on a single feature or bug fix.

218

4. **Code Reviews**:

   o Code reviews should be part of the Git workflow. Before merging changes into the main branch, pull requests (PRs) should be reviewed by other team members to ensure that code quality is maintained, bugs are caught early, and best practices are followed.

   o Pull requests should include a clear description of the changes and should be thoroughly tested before being merged.

5. **Use of `.gitignore`**:

   o Ensure that unnecessary files (such as build artifacts, logs, and IDE-specific files) are added to the `.gitignore` file. This keeps the repository clean and prevents unnecessary files from being committed.

6. **Tagging Releases**:

   o Use **Git tags** to mark specific points in the project, such as software releases or milestone versions. Tags provide a way to easily reference stable points in the project's history.

7. **Resolve Conflicts Early**:

o If merge conflicts occur, resolve them as soon as possible to avoid blocking other developers' work. Communicate with team members if conflicts are complex and require careful consideration.

Workflow Models: Git Flow, GitHub Flow, GitLab Flow

Various Git workflow models help teams coordinate development, manage releases, and handle parallel work. Three of the most commonly used workflow models are **Git Flow**, **GitHub Flow**, and **GitLab Flow**. Let's explore each of these models:

1. Git Flow

Git Flow is a branching model created by Vincent Driessen that defines a strict set of rules for managing branches in a Git repository. It is particularly useful for projects with **scheduled releases** and teams working on **multiple features** at once.

- **Main Branches**:
  - o **main**: This branch always contains the stable, production-ready code. All production releases come from this branch.

- o **develop**: This branch is used for integrating features and bug fixes. It contains the latest development changes and is the base branch for all feature and release branches.

- **Supporting Branches**:
  - o **Feature branches**: Created from `develop` for new features. Once a feature is completed, it is merged back into `develop`.

    bash

    ```
    git checkout -b feature/your-feature develop
    ```

  - o **Release branches**: Used for preparing new versions of the software. They are created from `develop` and are used for final testing, bug fixes, and preparing release notes. After the release, they are merged into both `main` and `develop`.

    bash

    ```
    git checkout -b release/1.0 develop
    ```

o **Hotfix branches**: Used to fix critical bugs in production. They are created from `main` and merged back into both `main` and `develop`.

```bash
git checkout -b hotfix/urgent-fix main
```

Pros:

- Clear structure and process for managing multiple features and releases.
- Great for projects with scheduled releases and multiple contributors.

Cons:

- Can be cumbersome for smaller teams or projects with continuous, rapid development.

---

2. GitHub Flow

GitHub Flow is a simplified Git workflow used primarily for **continuous delivery** and **continuous deployment**. It is ideal for smaller teams or projects that deploy frequently to production.

- **Main Branch**:
    - **main**: The `main` branch always contains the production-ready code. All changes are made via pull requests from feature branches to `main`.
- **Feature Branches**:
    - Developers create a new branch off of `main` for each feature or bug fix. Once the feature is complete, it is merged back into `main` through a pull request. Automated tests are run on the feature branch before merging.

    bash

    ```
    git checkout -b feature/your-feature
    main
    ```

    - Once the pull request is reviewed and passes all tests, it is merged into `main` and automatically deployed to production.

Pros:

- Simple and efficient for rapid development and deployment.

- Works well with **continuous deployment** where every change is deployed immediately.

Cons:

- Doesn't provide as much structure for managing releases and hotfixes as Git Flow does.

- Less suited for large projects with many developers.

3. GitLab Flow

GitLab Flow combines elements of both **Git Flow** and **GitHub Flow** and can be adapted for various development strategies. It's designed to integrate closely with GitLab's built-in CI/CD features.

- **Main Branches**:
  - o **main**: This branch contains the production-ready code and is used for continuous deployment.

224

- o **develop**: For teams using GitLab Flow, the develop branch is where most feature branches are merged before the final release.

- **Environment Branches**:
  - o **staging**: Used for pre-production testing. Code is deployed here first to test in an environment that mirrors production.
  - o **production**: For the live code that is deployed to production environments.

- **Feature and Issue Branches**:
  - o Developers create feature branches from main or develop and work on them until they are complete. Once the work is done, a merge request is created to merge the branch back into develop or main.

Pros:

- Flexible and works well for teams that need a combination of **CI/CD pipelines** and **structured releases**.
- Allows for parallel development in feature branches and testing in staging environments.

Cons:

- More complex than GitHub Flow, so it's better suited for larger projects or teams.

Real-World Example: Managing Multiple Developers on the Same Project Using a Well-defined Git Workflow

Scenario:

You are working on a **web application** with a team of developers. The team needs to manage multiple features, bug fixes, and releases. You decide to adopt **Git Flow** to streamline collaboration and ensure that your releases are well-managed.

1. **Step 1: Initialize Git Flow:**

    o You initialize Git Flow for the project:

    ```bash
    git flow init
    ```

    o Git Flow will automatically create the `main` and `develop` branches and set up the workflow for creating feature, release, and hotfix branches.

226

2. **Step 2: Working on Feature Branches**:

   o Developer A starts working on a new feature (e.g.,
     `user-authentication`) and creates a new
     feature branch:

     ```bash
     bash
     ```

     ```bash
     git flow feature start user-
     authentication
     ```

   o Developer B works on another feature (e.g.,
     `payment-integration`) and creates a separate
     feature branch:

     ```bash
     bash
     ```

     ```bash
     git flow feature start payment-
     integration
     ```

3. **Step 3: Merging Features Back into `develop`**:

   o After Developer A finishes their feature, they
     finish the feature and merge it back into
     `develop`:

     ```bash
     bash
     ```

```
git   flow   feature   finish   user-
authentication
```

o The merge automatically triggers testing to ensure that the new feature integrates properly with the existing code.

4. **Step 4: Creating a Release Branch**:

o When all features for the next version are ready, the team creates a release branch to prepare for production:

```bash

git flow release start 1.0.0
```

o The team tests the release branch, fixes any remaining issues, and merges the release branch into both main and develop.

5. **Step 5: Tagging the Release**:

o Once the release branch is merged, a tag is created to mark the version:

```bash

git flow release finish 1.0.0
```

6. **Step 6: Hotfixes**:

  o If a critical bug is discovered in production, a hotfix branch is created from `main`:

  ```bash
  git flow hotfix start fix-login-bug
  ```

  o After fixing the bug, the hotfix is merged back into `main` and `develop`, ensuring that the bug is resolved in both environments.

Key Takeaways:

- **Git Flow, GitHub Flow**, and **GitLab Flow** are popular Git workflow models that help teams collaborate efficiently, manage feature development, and ensure smooth releases.

- **Git Flow** provides a structured approach with dedicated branches for features, releases, and hotfixes, making it ideal for larger teams and projects with scheduled releases.

- **GitHub Flow** is simpler and works well for teams practicing continuous deployment and pushing updates directly to production.

- **GitLab Flow** offers flexibility by combining elements of both Git Flow and GitHub Flow, integrating well with GitLab's CI/CD tools.

- Using **Git workflows** ensures that your team can work collaboratively, manage releases, and maintain a stable codebase.

In the next chapter, we will explore **Git security practices**, focusing on securing your Git repositories, managing access, and protecting sensitive data.

CHAPTER 20

MANAGING LARGE TEAMS WITH GIT

Managing large teams in a Git-based project presents unique challenges. With many developers working on different features, fixing bugs, and collaborating simultaneously, it's crucial to establish strong collaboration practices, effective **branching strategies**, and clear **permissions management**. Additionally, integrating Git with **issue tracking tools** can help streamline workflows and enhance team communication. In this chapter, we'll explore **advanced collaboration techniques** for large teams, including **branching strategies**, **permissions**, and integration with issue tracking tools, and walk through a **real-world example** of managing an enterprise-level project with Git.

Advanced Collaboration Techniques for Large Teams

Collaboration in large teams requires more than just basic Git knowledge; it involves creating clear workflows, ensuring that developers work in parallel without causing conflicts, and

231

managing the repository's health. Here are some techniques for managing collaboration effectively:

1. **Establishing Clear Commit and Branching Conventions**:

   o Define rules for **commit messages** and **branch naming conventions** to ensure consistency and clarity across the repository. For example:

     ▪ Commit messages should follow the format: `[TYPE] [Ticket ID] - [Short Description]`, where `TYPE` might be `Feature`, `Fix`, `Docs`, etc.

     ▪ Branches should be named based on the type of work, e.g., `feature/login-form`, `bugfix/payment-bug`, `hotfix/security-patch`.

2. **Code Reviews and Pull Requests**:

   o Implement a strict **pull request** (PR) review process. Developers should always create PRs for their changes and request reviews from team members. Code reviews ensure that new changes meet the project's quality standards, catch bugs early, and encourage knowledge sharing among team members.

o Set up **CI/CD** pipelines that automatically run tests on PRs to ensure that new changes do not break the build.

3. **Frequent Synchronization**:

o Encourage developers to **sync frequently** with the main branch (`main` or `develop`) to keep their local branches up-to-date and avoid conflicts. This can be achieved using the **rebase** strategy (e.g., `git pull --rebase`) instead of merge to maintain a cleaner commit history.

4. **Feature Toggles/Flags**:

o For large-scale features that may take time to develop, consider using **feature toggles/flags** to allow partial features to be merged into the main branch without affecting users. This allows teams to integrate new features incrementally without delaying other work.

5. **Conflict Resolution Strategy**:

o Establish clear procedures for resolving **merge conflicts**. Encourage team members to resolve conflicts quickly and to communicate effectively when conflicts arise, particularly if they involve large, complex changes.

Permissions, Branching Strategies, and Integration with Issue Tracking Tools

1. **Managing Permissions in Git Repositories**:

   o   For larger teams, it's important to manage access to different parts of the repository to ensure that sensitive or critical components are not modified by unauthorized team members.

   o   **GitHub**, **GitLab**, and **Bitbucket** provide robust permission systems that allow repository owners to control who can access the repository, who can commit to certain branches, and who can merge pull requests.

   ▪ **Read Access**: Allows users to clone and view the repository.

   ▪ **Write Access**: Allows users to contribute code via branches, commits, and PRs.

- **Admin Access**: Grants full control over repository settings, including permissions, branch protection, and integrations.
   o You can implement **branch protection rules** to prevent direct commits to critical branches (e.g., `main`), enforcing a policy where changes must go through pull requests and be reviewed before merging.

2. **Branching Strategies**:
   o Large teams benefit from clear and consistent **branching strategies** to avoid chaos in the repository. Some popular strategies include:
   o **Git Flow**:
      - As discussed earlier, **Git Flow** is perfect for larger teams working on features, hotfixes, and releases. It uses multiple branches such as `main`, `develop`, `feature`, `release`, and `hotfix`.
      - Developers work on feature branches (`feature/xyz`) and submit them for review and merging into the `develop`

branch. The `develop` branch serves as the integration branch, where all feature branches are merged before being released.

- **GitHub Flow**:
  - For teams that prioritize continuous deployment, **GitHub Flow** is a simpler approach. Developers work directly on feature branches created off `main` and open pull requests to merge their changes back into `main`.
  - This flow is ideal for teams deploying frequently to production.
- **Trunk-Based Development**:
  - In **Trunk-Based Development**, developers work directly on a single branch (often called `main` or `trunk`) and continuously push small, incremental changes to it. This approach requires strong automated testing and frequent commits.

236

- This strategy is useful for teams practicing **continuous delivery** and **continuous integration** where fast, small changes are prioritized.

3. **Integration with Issue Tracking Tools**:

   o Git integrates seamlessly with **issue tracking tools** (e.g., **Jira, GitHub Issues, GitLab Issues**) to provide visibility and better management of work tasks. Linking Git commits, branches, and pull requests to issues ensures that everyone in the team knows what work is being done, its progress, and its impact.

   Example Workflow with Jira:

   o In your **commit messages**, include the Jira issue ID to associate commits with specific tasks. For instance:

   bash

   ```
   git commit -m "[TASK-123] Fix authentication bug"
   ```

o This allows team members and project managers to track progress on issues and tasks directly within the version control system.

o Similarly, pull requests should be linked to issues to ensure that code changes are associated with the tasks they are solving. GitHub and GitLab allow automatic linking of PRs to issues by referencing the issue number in the PR description.

Real-World Example: Managing Enterprise-Level Projects with Git

Scenario:

You're working on an enterprise-level **web application** with a large development team spread across multiple regions. The team is using **Git Flow** as the main Git workflow, and the repository has grown to contain multiple components (e.g., frontend, backend, API services, and shared libraries).

1. **Step 1: Branch Structure Setup**:

   o You initialize **Git Flow** in the project to structure your branches:

238

```
bash

git flow init
```

- o This creates the main branches (`main`, `develop`) and sets up a framework for creating `feature`, `release`, and `hotfix` branches.

2. **Step 2: Managing Permissions**:

- o You assign **admin access** to core developers who can manage branches, settings, and integrations, while other team members receive **write access** to contribute code.

- o To ensure stability, you configure **branch protection rules** on the `main` and `develop` branches to enforce that all changes must go through pull requests and be reviewed by at least two senior developers before merging.

3. **Step 3: Issue Tracking Integration**:

- o The team uses **Jira** for issue tracking. Each feature or bug fix is tied to a Jira ticket, and the Jira issue ID is added to the commit messages and pull request descriptions.

- o For example, a commit might look like:

239

```bash
bash
```

```bash
git commit -m "[APP-123] Add user
authentication feature"
```

o   This makes it easy to track which code changes correspond to which tasks.

4.   **Step 4: Working with Feature Branches**:

o   Developers create **feature branches** off the `develop` branch for every new feature or bug fix. After the feature is completed, it is merged back into `develop` via a pull request.

o   For example, if Developer A is working on the **user authentication** feature, they create a feature branch:

```bash
bash
```

```bash
git flow feature start user-
authentication
```

5.   **Step 5: Regular Merging and Testing**:

o   Developers frequently **pull and rebase** changes from the `develop` branch to keep their feature branches up-to-date. This ensures that changes from other developers don't cause conflicts when merging.

```bash
git pull --rebase origin develop
```

o Once the feature is complete, Developer A creates a pull request to merge their feature branch back into `develop`. Automated tests are triggered on the pull request to ensure no issues are introduced.

6. **Step 6: Creating a Release Branch**:

o Once all features for the next release are merged into `develop`, the team creates a **release branch** to prepare for production:

```bash
git flow release start 1.0.0
```

o This branch undergoes final testing, and any last-minute bug fixes are made here before merging into `main`.

7. **Step 7: Merging and Deployment**:

o   After the release branch is tested and ready, it is merged into both `main` and `develop`, and a tag is created for version `1.0.0`:

bash

```
git flow release finish 1.0.0
```

o   The `main` branch is then automatically deployed to production, while the `develop` branch continues to be the source of new features.

Key Takeaways:

- **Effective collaboration** in large teams requires strong commit and branching conventions, frequent synchronization with the main branch, and a clear code review process.

- **Git Flow**, **GitHub Flow**, and **GitLab Flow** provide structured approaches for managing branching, releases, and hotfixes in larger teams.

- **Permissions management** ensures that only authorized team members can access and modify critical parts of the repository.

242

- Integrating **Git with issue tracking tools** like Jira or GitHub Issues provides visibility into the progress of work tasks and keeps the team aligned.

- Managing **enterprise-level projects** with Git requires efficient workflows, clear branching strategies, and seamless integration with CI/CD tools, automated testing, and issue tracking.

In the next chapter, we'll delve into **Git security practices**, covering how to protect your repository, manage credentials securely, and mitigate potential security risks.

CHAPTER 21

GIT AND AGILE DEVELOPMENT

In today's fast-paced software development environment, **Agile methodologies** have become the standard for managing projects. Agile emphasizes flexibility, collaboration, and delivering incremental value over time. **Git**, with its flexibility and distributed nature, integrates well with Agile practices, allowing teams to manage code effectively and support continuous delivery.

In this chapter, we will explore how to **integrate Git with Agile methodologies**, and how Git can be used for **sprint planning**, **task management**, and **code iteration**. Additionally, we'll provide a **real-world example** of how Git can be used to collaborate effectively in an Agile environment.

Integrating Git with Agile Methodologies

Agile development emphasizes **iterative progress**, **collaboration**, and **flexibility**. Git, as a version control system, helps facilitate

Agile principles by allowing teams to manage code efficiently in parallel development environments. Here are some ways to integrate Git with Agile methodologies:

1. **Feature Branching for Incremental Development**:
   - In Agile, work is broken down into small, manageable tasks or **user stories**, which are completed within **sprints** (typically two to four weeks). Git's branching capabilities support this by allowing developers to work on isolated **feature branches** for each user story or task.
   - Each feature branch corresponds to a **user story** or task, and it can be merged into the main development branch (usually `develop`) after the feature is complete and tested.

2. **Commit Frequency and Small Iterations**:
   - Agile encourages teams to deliver work frequently and in small iterations. Git's support for **frequent commits** ensures that developers can commit their work regularly, making it easier to track progress and integrate changes continuously.

245

o The goal is to keep commits small and focused on a specific piece of functionality or bug fix. This minimizes conflicts and makes it easier to review changes.

3. **Continuous Integration and Testing**:

   o **Continuous Integration (CI)** is a key practice in Agile, where developers frequently merge their changes into the shared codebase, typically multiple times a day. Git, combined with CI tools like **Jenkins, Travis CI**, or **GitHub Actions**, helps automate the testing process for each commit, ensuring that the code is always in a deployable state.

   o Each time a developer pushes their feature branch to the repository, the CI pipeline runs automated tests to check for integration issues or bugs.

4. **Collaborative Pull Requests**:

   o Agile emphasizes **collaboration** between developers, QA, and other stakeholders. Git supports collaboration through **pull requests**, where team members can review each other's code before merging it into the main branch.

o In an Agile setting, pull requests are often linked to **user stories** or **tasks**, ensuring that work is tied to specific deliverables within the sprint.

5. **Tracking Progress with Git and Issue Tracking Tools**:

o **Issue tracking systems** (e.g., **Jira, GitHub Issues, GitLab Issues**) integrate well with Git to manage tasks, user stories, and bugs. Git commit messages and pull requests can reference specific issues or tickets, allowing team members and managers to track progress on the project.

o For example, a commit message might include the issue ID like so: `git commit -m "[ISSUE-123] Implement user login feature"`, making it easy to trace changes back to specific tasks.

Using Git for Sprint Planning, Task Management, and Code Iteration

1. **Sprint Planning**:

o At the start of each sprint, the development team gathers to plan the tasks that need to be completed. Git plays a critical role by providing the structure for organizing code changes through branches.

o Each task or **user story** is typically assigned to a separate **feature branch**. The team decides which user stories are prioritized for the sprint and assigns them to the corresponding branches.

Example: In a sprint planning session, the team decides that the following features should be developed:

o **User authentication** (assigned to feature/user-authentication).

o **Payment gateway integration** (assigned to feature/payment-gateway).

o Each developer creates a new branch for their assigned tasks:

bash

```
git checkout -b feature/user-authentication
git checkout -b feature/payment-gateway
```

2. **Task Management**:

    o   Git integrates well with **issue tracking tools** to track the status of tasks and user stories. Each feature branch is linked to a task in the issue tracker, and pull requests are used to manage code reviews and merges.

    o   For instance, using **Jira** or **GitHub Issues**, each task or user story can be given a status (e.g., **To Do**, **In Progress**, **In Review**, **Done**). Git branches and commits are then used to update the status of these tasks.

    Example: In Jira, the task `USER-123` for **user authentication** is marked as "In Progress" when the developer starts working on it. When the developer finishes, they create a pull request to merge the `feature/user-authentication` branch into `develop`, and the task status is updated to "In Review."

3. **Code Iteration**:

    o   Agile emphasizes **rapid iteration**, and Git facilitates this by allowing easy branching, merging, and rebasing. Developers can iteratively

249

implement features or bug fixes, make frequent commits, and continually improve the code.

o   As part of each iteration, developers frequently pull the latest changes from the `develop` branch to ensure their feature is up-to-date and to minimize merge conflicts.

Example: Developer A works on the **user authentication feature** in the `feature/user-authentication` branch. After making significant progress, they regularly pull from the `develop` branch to keep their code up-to-date:

```bash
```

```bash
git pull --rebase origin develop
```

This keeps the branch in sync with the rest of the project and prevents issues when merging the feature back into `develop`.

Real-World Example: Collaborating in an Agile Environment with Git

Scenario:

You are working in a medium-sized team on a **web application**. The team follows Agile practices, and you are using **Git Flow** as your Git workflow. The project has a `main` branch for production-ready code and a `develop` branch for integrating new features. Each developer works on their own feature branch, and all tasks are tracked in **Jira**.

1. **Step 1: Sprint Planning**:
   - At the start of the sprint, the team identifies the user stories and tasks to be completed. These tasks are linked to **Jira issues**. For example, the sprint backlog includes:
     - **USER-101**: Implement user registration form.
     - **USER-102**: Integrate Google login.
     - **USER-103**: Fix bug in the payment form.

2. **Step 2: Creating Feature Branches**:
   - The development team creates feature branches based on the tasks:

```bash
git checkout -b feature/user-
registration develop
git checkout -b feature/google-login
develop
git checkout -b bugfix/payment-bug
develop
```

- o Each branch corresponds to a Jira issue, and the developers begin working on their assigned tasks.

3. **Step 3: Daily Standups**:

- o During daily standups, developers update the team on their progress, any blockers, and share insights on the work they are doing. If any issues arise during development, such as merge conflicts or bugs, they are addressed immediately.

4. **Step 4: Pull Requests and Code Reviews**:

- o As the developers complete their tasks, they create **pull requests** to merge their feature branches into develop. Each pull request is linked to the corresponding Jira issue (e.g., **USER-101** for the registration form feature).

- o Team members review the pull request, check the code, and run automated tests to ensure quality.

After a successful review, the branch is merged into `develop`.

5. **Step 5: Sprint Review and Demo**:

   o At the end of the sprint, the team conducts a sprint review and demo. The completed features are tested in a staging environment, and stakeholders are shown the new features that were developed.

6. **Step 6: Sprint Retrospective**:

   o In the sprint retrospective, the team reflects on the sprint and discusses what went well, what could be improved, and any challenges faced during development. Git workflows, code reviews, and pull request processes are often part of the discussion to ensure the team is collaborating efficiently.

Key Takeaways:

- **Git** integrates well with **Agile methodologies**, supporting iterative development and collaborative workflows.

- **Feature branches** enable developers to work on small, manageable tasks, with each branch typically corresponding to a user story or task in the project.

- **Pull requests** facilitate **code reviews**, ensuring that new code is thoroughly reviewed and tested before merging into the main branch.

- Git's flexibility supports various branching models (e.g., **Git Flow**) that help manage releases, hotfixes, and new features in an organized way.

- Integration with **issue tracking tools** like **Jira** or **GitHub Issues** ensures that tasks and user stories are tracked and linked directly to the code.

In the next chapter, we will explore **Git performance tuning** and how to optimize Git operations for larger teams and projects, focusing on strategies for managing big repositories and maintaining efficient workflows.

CHAPTER 22

TROUBLESHOOTING COMMON

GIT PROBLEMS

Git is a powerful tool, but like any complex system, users occasionally encounter problems. Whether you're dealing with **merge conflicts, lost commits, untracked files,** or other issues, it's important to know how to troubleshoot and resolve common Git problems effectively. In this chapter, we'll explore how to resolve some of the most common Git issues, recover from mistakes using **Git's reflog,** and undo changes. We'll also walk through a **real-world example** of fixing a broken commit history.

Resolving Common Issues in Git

1. **Merge Conflicts**:

   o **Merge conflicts** occur when Git is unable to automatically merge two branches because changes made in one branch are in conflict with changes made in another branch. These conflicts need to be resolved manually by the developer.

How to resolve merge conflicts:

o When a merge conflict occurs, Git will mark the conflicting files and add conflict markers (e.g., <<<<<<<, =======, >>>>>>>) to the files in question.

o Open the conflicting files and decide whether to:

  ▪ Keep changes from your branch (above =======).

  ▪ Keep changes from the other branch (below =======).

  ▪ Combine both changes if necessary.

o After resolving the conflict, remove the conflict markers and save the file.

o Stage the resolved files:

```bash

git add <resolved-file>
```

o Commit the merge:

```bash
```

256

```
git    commit   -m   "Resolved   merge
conflict in <file>"
```

2. **Lost Commits**:

   o   Sometimes, commits can seem lost if you accidentally delete a branch or if a merge is done incorrectly. Fortunately, **Git reflog** helps you recover lost commits.

   Using Git Reflog to Recover Lost Commits:

   o   **git reflog** is a command that allows you to see the history of your **HEAD** (your current branch), including commits that may no longer be part of the current branch's history. This makes it a powerful tool for recovering lost commits.

   o   Run git reflog to see the list of recent actions:

   bash

   ```
   git reflog
   ```

   o   You'll see a list of commits with their corresponding reference points (e.g., HEAD@{0}, HEAD@{1}, etc.).

257

- To recover a lost commit, you can check out the commit hash from `reflog` and create a new branch or reset your current branch to that commit:

  bash

  ```
  git    checkout    -b    <new-branch>
  <commit-hash>
  ```

3. **Untracked Files**:
   - Git marks files as **untracked** if they are not yet added to the repository. Untracked files do not get committed until they are added with `git add`.

   How to handle untracked files:

   - Use `git status` to see a list of untracked files.

     bash

     ```
     git status
     ```

   - To add an untracked file to Git:

     bash

```
git add <file>
```

o   To remove untracked files (if you no longer need them), you can use:

```
bash
```

```
git clean -f
```

Recovering from Mistakes: Git's Reflog and Undoing Changes

Git provides several mechanisms for undoing changes or recovering from mistakes. Here are some ways to handle common mistakes:

1.   **Undoing the Last Commit**:

   o   If you've committed changes and want to undo the commit, you can use the following commands depending on whether you want to keep or discard the changes.

   o   To undo the last commit but **keep the changes** in the working directory (i.e., as uncommitted changes):

```
bash
```

```
git reset --soft HEAD~1
```

o   To undo the last commit and **discard the changes** entirely:

```
bash
```

```
git reset --hard HEAD~1
```

2.   **Reverting a Commit:**

o   If you want to undo a commit but still keep the history intact (especially useful in collaborative projects), you can use the `git revert` command to create a new commit that undoes the changes made in a previous commit.

```
bash
```

```
git revert <commit-hash>
```

o   This will create a new commit that reverts the changes introduced by the specified commit.

3.   **Undoing Staged Changes:**

o If you've added changes to the staging area (`git add`) but haven't committed yet and want to unstage them:

```bash
git reset HEAD <file>
```

4. **Restoring Deleted Files**:

o If you accidentally deleted a file and want to restore it from the last commit, you can use:

```bash
git checkout -- <file>
```

Real-World Example: Fixing a Broken Commit History

Scenario:

You've been working on a feature branch (`feature/user-authentication`) for a few days, but you realize that the commits you've made are disorganized. Some of your commits include a mix of unrelated changes, and you want to clean up the commit history before merging it into the `develop` branch.

261

Step 1: Review the Commit History:

- Use `git log` to review the commit history and identify which commits need to be changed.

```bash
```

```bash
git log --oneline
```

Step 2: Interactive Rebase:

- Use **interactive rebase** to clean up the commit history. This allows you to **reorder**, **combine** (`squash`), or **edit** commits before pushing them to the remote repository.
- Run the following command to start an interactive rebase for the last N commits (e.g., the last 5 commits):

```bash
```

```bash
git rebase -i HEAD~5
```

- This will open an editor with a list of commits:

```plaintext
```

```plaintext
pick e3a1b35 Implement login form
pick d45f2d7 Fix issue with form validation
```

```
pick    9b2aee1    Add    password    reset
functionality
pick 1f93b72 Update login styles
pick b71a4d0 Add tests for authentication
feature
```

- You can now:

  - **Reorder** commits by changing the order of the lines.

  - **Squash** commits by replacing `pick` with `squash` (e.g., if you want to combine the login form commit with the form validation fix).

  - **Edit** a commit by changing `pick` to `edit`.

Step 3: Apply the Changes:

- After saving and closing the editor, Git will apply the changes, potentially prompting you to resolve conflicts if necessary. You can continue the rebase process by using:

```
bash

git rebase --continue
```

Step 4: Push the Changes:

263

- Once the rebase is complete, you will have a cleaner commit history. If you've already pushed the original commits to a remote repository, you will need to force push the changes to update the history:

```bash
git push --force
```

Key Takeaways:

- **Merge conflicts** are common when working in teams, but they can be resolved by manually editing conflicting files and staging the changes.
- **Lost commits** can often be recovered using **Git's reflog**, which provides a history of recent changes to the HEAD.
- **Untracked files** can be managed using `git status`, `git add`, and `git clean`.
- Git provides several ways to **undo changes**, including **resetting commits**, **reverting commits**, and **restoring files**.

- **Interactive rebase** allows you to clean up your commit history, making it easier to merge changes into the main branches without introducing unnecessary noise.

- Regularly **reviewing and cleaning** up your commit history ensures that your Git repository remains manageable and your version history is clear.

In the next chapter, we will discuss **Git best practices** for maintaining a healthy repository and working efficiently with your team, ensuring consistent quality and streamlined collaboration.

CHAPTER 23

BEST PRACTICES FOR GIT USAGE

Git is a fundamental tool for modern software development, and maintaining a clean, efficient, and organized workflow is essential for both individual developers and large teams. Best practices for **commit messages, branching**, and **merging** can significantly improve the collaboration process, making it easier to understand the history of a project, track progress, and integrate new features. In this chapter, we will discuss **best practices** for Git usage, focusing on **commit messages**, **branching**, **merging**, and organizing your repository for better collaboration. Additionally, we'll walk through a **real-world example** of maintaining a clean and organized Git history to benefit future developers.

Best Practices for Writing Commit Messages

Clear and descriptive **commit messages** are critical for understanding the project's history and making collaboration easier. Here are some best practices for writing commit messages:

1. **Use the Imperative Mood**:

   o Commit messages should describe what the commit does, not what it did. The imperative mood is standard practice for Git commit messages. For example:

     ▪ Correct: `Add login feature`

     ▪ Incorrect: `Added login feature`

2. **Write a Short, Descriptive Subject Line**:

   o The subject line should briefly describe the changes (usually under 50 characters). It should be concise but informative enough to understand the commit's purpose at a glance.

3. **Include a Detailed Body (if necessary)**:

   o If the commit requires more explanation (e.g., why a change was made or how the change was implemented), include a body after the subject line. Separate the subject and body with a blank line.

   o Keep the body under 72 characters per line to maintain readability in various Git tools and interfaces.

Example:

```
bash

git commit -m "Fix user authentication bug

The user authentication process was failing
due to an incorrect token validation. Fixed
the bug by updating the validation function
to check the token format."
```

4. **Be Specific and Avoid Vagueness:**

    o   Commit messages should be specific and avoid vague terms like "fix", "improve", or "update" without further clarification. Instead of writing "fix bug," describe what bug was fixed and how.

   Example:

    o   Instead of: `Fix bug`
    o   Use: `Fix bug that caused incorrect token validation in authentication`

5. **Use Commit Messages to Group Related Changes:**

    o   Each commit should represent a logical unit of work. Group related changes into a single commit, and avoid committing unrelated changes together. This makes the history more readable and makes it easier to revert or adjust individual changes.

Best Practices for Branching and Merging

Effective **branching** and **merging** strategies ensure that your codebase remains stable and clean, even when multiple developers are working in parallel.

1. **Work in Feature Branches**:
   o Each feature, bug fix, or enhancement should be developed in its own **feature branch**. This isolates changes and keeps the main branch (`main` or `develop`) stable.
   o Naming conventions for feature branches can help identify the purpose of the branch. For example:
     ▪ `feature/user-login`
     ▪ `bugfix/payment-bug`
     ▪ `hotfix/crash-on-launch`
2. **Keep Feature Branches Short-lived**:
   o Avoid keeping feature branches open for too long. The longer a branch remains open, the

more difficult it becomes to integrate it back into the main branch due to the potential for conflicts.

o   Aim to finish a feature and merge it back to the `develop` or `main` branch within a few days.

3.   **Regularly Sync with the Main Branch**:

o   Regularly sync your feature branch with the main development branch (`main` or `develop`) to stay up-to-date with changes made by other developers.

   ▪   Pull from the main branch frequently:

```bash

git pull --rebase origin develop
```

   ▪   This keeps your feature branch up-to-date, minimizing merge conflicts and preventing large, complex merges at the end of a development cycle.

4.   **Avoid Merging to `main` Directly**:

o   Never merge directly into the `main` branch without proper review. Instead, use **pull requests** (or **merge requests**) to ensure code is reviewed, tested, and validated before merging.

- o Use **branch protection rules** to enforce this workflow and require pull requests for merges to the `main` branch.

5. **Use Git Merge or Rebase Correctly**:

- o **Merge** is the most straightforward way to combine branches, preserving the full history of the changes. Use merge for integrating features and bug fixes into the main branch.

```bash

git checkout develop
git merge feature/user-login
```

- o **Rebase** is useful for maintaining a clean, linear history by "replaying" your feature branch's commits onto the latest `main` branch, avoiding merge commits.

```bash

git pull --rebase origin develop
```

    o   Rebase is particularly useful for cleaning up your commit history before merging into `develop` or `main`.

Organizing Your Repository for Better Collaboration

Organizing your Git repository and establishing a collaborative environment is key to ensuring smooth workflows for large teams. Here are some tips for organizing your repository effectively:

1. **Create a Clear Directory Structure**:
   - o Organize your repository's directories logically, grouping related files together. For example, you might have:
     - `src/` for source code
     - `docs/` for documentation
     - `tests/` for test files
     - `scripts/` for utility scripts
   - o Having a consistent structure helps new contributors navigate the project easily.

2. **Use `.gitignore`**:

o Add a `.gitignore` file to prevent unnecessary files (such as build artifacts, IDE configuration files, or temporary files) from being tracked by Git. This keeps the repository clean and ensures only relevant files are versioned.

o Popular `.gitignore` templates can be found on **GitHub's gitignore repository**.

3. **Document Your Workflow and Guidelines**:

o Maintain a **CONTRIBUTING.md** file with detailed guidelines for developers on how to contribute to the project. This should include instructions on:

- How to fork the repository and create feature branches.

- How to format commit messages.

- How to submit pull requests.

- How to run tests and check code quality.

o Also, document the Git workflow your team is following (e.g., Git Flow, GitHub Flow).

4. **Tag Important Releases**:

o Use Git **tags** to mark significant versions of your project, such as production releases, major milestones, or feature completions. This allows developers to easily refer to specific versions of the project.

- o Example:

```bash

git tag -a v1.0.0 -m "First official release"
git push origin v1.0.0
```

Real-World Example: Maintaining a Clean and Organized Git History for Future Developers

Scenario:

You are leading a development team on a large enterprise-level project with several components, including a web frontend, API backend, and shared libraries. Your goal is to ensure the project's Git history remains clean, organized, and understandable for future developers.

1. **Step 1: Establish a Git Workflow**:
   - o You decide to use **Git Flow** as the team's workflow, ensuring that all feature work is done

in feature branches, releases are created from release branches, and hotfixes are made on hotfix branches.

2. **Step 2: Branch Management**:

   o Developers are instructed to create feature branches for each new task, and each feature branch is linked to a Jira ticket or GitHub issue. For example, Developer A is working on the **user authentication** feature and creates a feature branch:

   bash

   ```
   git checkout -b feature/user-authentication develop
   ```

   o The developer commits changes frequently with clear, descriptive commit messages:

   bash

   ```
   git commit -m "[FEATURE-123] Implement user login form"
   ```

3. **Step 3: Code Review and Pull Requests**:

o Once the feature is complete, Developer A creates a pull request to merge the feature branch into `develop`. The pull request includes a clear description of the changes and is reviewed by peers.

o Automated tests are triggered on the pull request to ensure that no new issues are introduced.

4. **Step 4: Merging and Tagging**:

o After successful testing and review, the pull request is merged into the `develop` branch using a merge commit. A release candidate is created using a `release` branch and tagged with a version number:

bash

```
git flow release start 1.0.0
git flow release finish 1.0.0
git tag -a v1.0.0 -m "First stable
release"
```

5. **Step 5: Cleaning Up Old Branches**:

o After features are merged, old feature branches are deleted both locally and remotely:

```
bash

git    branch    -d    feature/user-
authentication
git    push    origin    --delete
feature/user-authentication
```

6. **Step 6: Documentation**:

   o A **README.md** and **CONTRIBUTING.md** are maintained, explaining how to clone the repository, work with branches, and submit pull requests. The Git workflow is clearly documented to ensure consistency across the team.

Key Takeaways:

- **Git commit messages** should be clear, concise, and written in the imperative mood, describing what the commit does rather than what it did.

- **Branching** strategies like **Git Flow** provide structure for managing features, releases, and hotfixes, ensuring parallel development without disrupting the main codebase.

277

- Keep your **repository organized** with clear directory structures, `.gitignore` files, and detailed documentation to facilitate collaboration and maintainability.

- **Pull requests** and **code reviews** ensure that the codebase remains high quality and that all changes are properly reviewed before being merged.

- Maintaining a **clean Git history** by regularly merging, tagging releases, and removing unnecessary branches helps ensure future developers can easily navigate the codebase.

In the next chapter, we'll explore **advanced Git configurations** and how to customize your Git setup for enhanced productivity and team collaboration.

CHAPTER 24

THE FUTURE OF VERSION CONTROL SYSTEMS

Version control systems (VCS) have been a cornerstone of modern software development, enabling teams to collaborate efficiently, track code changes, and manage different versions of software. Git, as the most widely adopted VCS, has shaped how developers approach collaboration, code review, and continuous integration. As technology and software development practices evolve, so too must version control systems. This chapter will explore the **trends in version control**, the **innovations in Git**, and what the **future** might hold for Git and VCS in general. We'll also provide a **real-world example** of how teams can prepare for the next generation of version control systems.

Trends in Version Control: The Rise of Distributed Systems and New Tools

1. **Rise of Distributed Version Control Systems (DVCS):**

o The traditional **centralized version control systems** (CVCS), where all code is stored on a single central server, have largely been replaced by **distributed version control systems (DVCS)** like Git. DVCSs offer significant advantages in terms of flexibility, fault tolerance, and collaboration, making them ideal for modern, geographically distributed teams.

o In a **DVCS**, every developer has a local of the repository, including its full history. This allows developers to work offline and provides more resilient systems, as changes are not dependent on a central server.

Future Trend: The trend towards distributed systems is likely to continue, with more sophisticated tools being built to handle massive scale and offer seamless collaboration between distributed teams. Even for large organizations with complex, multi-team environments, Git's distributed nature offers a compelling advantage.

2. **New Version Control Tools and Ecosystems**:

- o While Git is the dominant version control system, there are newer tools and ecosystems that aim to either complement Git or offer alternative approaches. Some examples include:

  - **Mercurial**: Another distributed version control system that is more lightweight than Git but offers similar features.

  - **Perforce Helix Core**: A centralized version control system designed for large-scale enterprise teams, with a focus on performance and handling massive binary assets (often used in game development).

  - **Fossil**: A distributed VCS that includes integrated bug tracking, a wiki, and a web interface.

Future Trend: Version control tools will continue to evolve and specialize based on the needs of specific industries (e.g., game development, enterprise systems, etc.). We may see more hybrid systems or integrations that combine the strengths of Git with tools focused on specific workflows or data types.

3. **Version Control for Large-Scale Projects**:

    o   As projects grow larger in size, developers need tools that can handle complex workflows, manage large codebases, and support large teams across the globe. While Git has proven to be highly scalable, the demand for better scalability and performance will drive improvements.

    o   New solutions are emerging to help teams with extremely large repositories (like Facebook or Google), including **monorepo** management tools and solutions for optimizing Git performance (e.g., **Git LFS** for managing large binary files).

Future Trend: Expect continued efforts to enhance Git's ability to handle large repositories, with innovations that focus on performance, conflict resolution, and real-time collaboration in massive projects.

Innovations in Git: Enhancements and Upcoming Features

As the most popular version control system, Git is continually evolving. Some key enhancements and features that have been introduced or are expected to be introduced include:

1. **Git Performance Improvements**:
   o Git has made significant strides in performance over the years, and this trend is likely to continue, especially for large repositories. Some Git operations, such as cloning a large repository or checking out branches, can still be slow.
   o **Future Innovations**: Git developers are focusing on improving performance for **large repositories, reducing disk space usage**, and making the operations faster and more efficient. Future releases might include improvements to optimize workflows in teams working on huge codebases or managing millions of commits.

2. **GitHub Copilot and AI Integration**:
   o **GitHub Copilot**, powered by AI, offers suggestions for code as developers write, based on patterns it learned from millions of open-source

repositories. GitHub Copilot is only the beginning of what AI can do for version control.

- o **Future Innovations**: Git and other version control systems are likely to see deeper integrations with AI, offering capabilities such as **automated commit message generation, bug identification, code suggestions**, and **intelligent conflict resolution**.

3. **Better Merge and Conflict Resolution Tools**:

- o **Merge conflicts** are one of the most challenging aspects of collaborative work in Git. While Git has excellent tools for resolving conflicts, there's room for improvement in making the process smoother, especially in large teams.

- o **Future Innovations**: We could see more advanced tools for **automated conflict resolution, merge conflict prediction**, and **visual conflict resolution** to reduce the manual effort required during the merge process.

4. **Advanced Workflow Integration**:

- o Git workflows like **Git Flow** and **GitHub Flow** help structure development processes, but there are still many challenges with managing workflows in large, complex projects.

o **Future Innovations**: Version control systems will continue to improve their ability to integrate with **CI/CD pipelines, issue tracking systems, code quality tools**, and **project management tools**, allowing for more streamlined and automated development cycles.

5. **Security and Audit Features**:

o As security continues to be a major concern in software development, Git will likely evolve to include more advanced features for securing codebases and auditing changes. Features such as **signed commits** and **audit trails** already exist in Git, but further innovations are expected.

o **Future Innovations**: Expect more robust features around **access control**, **audit logs**, and **compliance tracking**, enabling teams to securely manage and track every change in the codebase.

Real-World Example: Preparing for the Next Generation of Version Control Systems

Scenario:

You're working as part of a **large development team** on an enterprise-level project. The project has grown substantially over the last few years, and your team faces challenges related to Git performance, large binary file management, and workflow efficiency. You're tasked with preparing your team for the next generation of version control systems.

1. **Step 1: Monitoring Git Performance**:

   o As your codebase grows, you notice that certain Git operations (e.g., cloning the repository, switching branches) have become slower. To prepare for future performance challenges, you begin by **adopting Git LFS** for managing large binary files and reducing the size of the repository's history.

2. **Step 2: Exploring AI-Assisted Development Tools**:

   o Your team begins exploring tools like **GitHub Copilot** and other AI-powered coding assistants. These tools provide real-time suggestions and automate some aspects of code review and merging. The goal is to speed up development by reducing manual review time and providing developers with smart code completion suggestions.

3. **Step 3: Enhancing Collaboration with Better Tools**:

   o You start using a combination of Git and **CI/CD pipelines** to automate your integration and deployment processes. You also integrate **Git** with your **issue tracking system** (e.g., Jira) and **project management tools** to link commits and pull requests with tasks and user stories.

4. **Step 4: Introducing Better Conflict Resolution Mechanisms**:

   o Recognizing that merge conflicts are a significant pain point, your team starts using **third-party Git merge tools** (such as **KDiff3** or **Beyond Compare**) and integrating them into your Git workflows. Additionally, you start exploring tools that provide **visual conflict resolution** to reduce the complexity of merging large codebases.

5. **Step 5: Preparing for the Future of Git**:

- o To stay ahead of future version control innovations, your team begins keeping an eye on upcoming features in Git and other version control systems. For instance, you subscribe to updates from the **Git mailing list** and **GitHub** to stay informed about potential **performance improvements, AI-powered features,** and **enhanced security**.

- o You also begin experimenting with **new version control tools** (like **Perforce Helix Core**) to see if they might provide benefits for your workflow.

Key Takeaways:

- **Distributed Version Control Systems (DVCS)**, like Git, will continue to rise in popularity due to their flexibility, fault tolerance, and ability to handle complex workflows across distributed teams.

- **Git innovations** will focus on performance, AI-powered development tools, better conflict resolution, and tighter integration with **CI/CD pipelines, issue tracking systems,** and **project management tools**.

- **Preparing for the future** means keeping an eye on emerging tools, workflows, and technologies to ensure your version control system scales as your project grows.

- **AI-assisted development tools** like **GitHub Copilot** are only the beginning of how version control systems will evolve, automating tasks and making collaboration even more efficient.

- **Security** will continue to be a major focus, with more features to manage access control, audit logs, and compliance tracking in version control systems.

In the next chapter, we will explore **advanced Git configurations** and how you can optimize your Git setup to improve performance, productivity, and collaboration across your team.

CHAPTER 25

BEYOND GIT: OTHER VERSION CONTROL SYSTEMS

While **Git** has become the dominant version control system (VCS) in modern software development, it is not the only VCS available. Other tools like **Mercurial** and **Subversion (SVN)** have also been widely used in various industries. Each version control system (VCS) has its own strengths and weaknesses, and it's essential for developers to understand the differences and know when to use each system. This chapter will provide an overview of other popular version control systems, compare them to Git, and offer guidance on when to use each. We'll also walk through a **real-world example** of transitioning from other version control systems to Git.

Overview of Other Popular Version Control Systems

1. **Mercurial (Hg):**

    o **Mercurial** is a distributed version control system, similar to Git, designed to handle large projects efficiently. It was developed to be easy to use, scalable, and fast.

- **Key Features**:
  - Distributed architecture, meaning every developer has a local of the repository.
  - Simple command set, making it easy for beginners to learn.
  - Excellent handling of large codebases, especially in enterprise-level projects.
  - Strong support for branching and merging, though not as flexible as Git.

- **Use Cases**: Mercurial is a popular choice for teams that require a distributed version control system but find Git's complexity overwhelming. It's often used in certain open-source projects and some enterprise systems.

2. **Subversion (SVN)**:

  - **Subversion (SVN)** is a centralized version control system (CVCS), where the repository is stored on a central server, and developers check out copies of the code to work on locally.

  - **Key Features**:

- Centralized model, where the entire repository is managed on a single server.

- Simpler branching and merging model compared to Git, but with more rigid workflows.

- Better suited for workflows where a centralized, controlled repository is preferred.

- Strong access control, making it easier to manage large teams with strict permissions.

o **Use Cases**: SVN is ideal for companies with a strict centralized workflow or when managing legacy projects. It is commonly used in industries where controlling access to the repository is critical, such as in government or large-scale enterprise systems.

3. **Perforce Helix Core**:

o **Perforce Helix Core** is an enterprise-class version control system optimized for handling large codebases and binary assets. It is particularly popular in industries like gaming and multimedia, where large binary files and assets are common.

- o **Key Features**:
  - Centralized VCS with excellent handling of large binary files.
  - Highly scalable and efficient, with support for large repositories and multiple teams.
  - Integrated with a variety of development tools and services.
- o **Use Cases**: Perforce is best suited for teams working on projects with massive amounts of binary assets, such as video games or large enterprise software with numerous assets.

4. **Fossil**:
   - o **Fossil** is a distributed version control system that includes built-in bug tracking, wiki, and web interface features.
   - o **Key Features**:
     - A simple, lightweight system that combines version control, bug tracking, and project management in a single tool.

293

- Ideal for small to medium-sized projects where an all-in-one tool is desired.

  o **Use Cases**: Fossil is often used by smaller teams or open-source projects that want a simple and lightweight version control system integrated with project management features.

Comparing Git to Other Systems and Knowing When to Use Each

When choosing a version control system, it's important to consider the specific needs of your team, project, and organization. Here's a comparison of Git to other popular VCS:

Feature	Git	Mercurial	Subversion (SVN)	Perforce	Fossil
Model	Distributed	Distributed	Centralized	Centralized	Distributed
Branching & Merging	Advanced, highly flexible	Simpler than Git	Simple, less	Strong branching support,	Simpler, less

294

Feature	Git	Mercurial	Subversion (SVN)	Perforce	Fossil
		but effective	flexible than Git	but flexible than Git	less flexible than Git
Performance with Large Repos	Good, optimized for many files	Good, but not as fast as Git	Slower with large repositories	Excellent, optimized for large repos	Good for small to medium repos
Ease of Use	More complex, but widely used	Easier to learn than Git	Easier to set up and use for beginners	Complex, more suited for enterprise	Simple and lightweight
Best Use Case	Open-source, large projects,	Smaller projects, user-	Legacy systems, centralized control	Large teams with binary	Small to medium-sized projects,

Feature	Git	Mercurial	Subversion (SVN)	Perforce	Fossil
	fast iterations	friendly for teams		assets (gaming, enterprise)	integrated tools

---

When to Use Each Version Control System

1. **Use Git When**:

   o You're working on **large, distributed teams**.

   o Your team needs a **flexible branching and merging model** that supports parallel development and rapid iterations.

   o You need **high performance with large projects**, especially with many contributors.

   o You're using **modern CI/CD pipelines** and tools that integrate well with Git (e.g., GitHub, GitLab, Bitbucket).

2. **Use Mercurial When**:

296

o   You want a **distributed version control system** but find Git's learning curve too steep.

o   You're working on a project with **moderate complexity** and need simplicity and reliability.

o   You are **migrating from other VCS** (such as Subversion) and need a simpler, more approachable system.

3. **Use Subversion (SVN) When:**

o   You need a **centralized version control system** with strict access control.

o   Your team is working on **legacy projects** or needs to maintain a **centralized workflow**.

o   You prefer **simple branching and merging** with fewer complexities.

4. **Use Perforce When:**

o   You're working on **projects with large binary assets**, such as video games or media files.

o   You need a system that can handle **massive codebases** with many contributors.

o   Your organization requires **enterprise-level scalability** and strong performance.

5. **Use Fossil When:**

o You need a **simple and lightweight version control system** that includes bug tracking and project management features.

o You're working on **small to medium-sized projects** and want an all-in-one solution.

Real-World Example: Transitioning from Other Version Control Systems to Git

Scenario:

Your team has been using **Subversion (SVN)** for several years to manage your software project. As the team has grown and your workflows have become more complex, you realize that **Git's distributed nature** and **advanced branching** features would be beneficial for your development process. The decision is made to **migrate from SVN to Git** to improve collaboration, scalability, and speed.

1. **Step 1: Evaluate the Project and Workflow:**

o Before migrating, you assess your project's structure and workflows. Your team needs to ensure that the migration won't interrupt ongoing development.

o The team is also concerned about the **learning curve** of Git, so you plan to conduct training sessions.

2. **Step 2: Set Up Git for the Project**:

o You create a new Git repository for the project and configure the **Git flow** workflow. You set up **branches** for development (`develop`), features (`feature/*`), releases (`release/*`), and hotfixes (`hotfix/*`).

o After configuring Git, you ensure that your project is properly structured, including **adding a** `.gitignore` **file** to ignore unnecessary files.

3. **Step 3: Migrate the Codebase**:

o You use a tool like **git-svn** to migrate your SVN repository to Git. This tool allows you to import your entire history of commits from SVN into Git.

```bash
```

```
git            svn            clone
https://svn.example.com/project/tru
nk
```

o After migration, all the code history is retained, and your team can begin using Git for future development.

4. **Step 4: Train the Team**:

o To ensure a smooth transition, you organize **training sessions** for the team, covering Git's basics like cloning, branching, committing, and pushing. You also introduce Git's **advanced features**, such as rebasing and handling merge conflicts.

5. **Step 5: Implement Git in the Development Workflow**:

o After migrating to Git, the team adopts Git Flow as their branching model. Developers start working on **feature branches** for each new task, ensuring that the main branch remains stable at all times.

o Pull requests (PRs) are used for code reviews, and automated testing is integrated into the CI/CD pipeline.

6. **Step 6: Review the Transition and Iterate:**

   o After a few months, you hold a **retrospective** to review how the transition to Git is going. The team shares feedback, and some issues with **merge conflicts** and **workflow inconsistencies** are identified. As a result, the team fine-tunes their Git practices to streamline the process further.

Key Takeaways:

- **Git** is a powerful, distributed version control system ideal for modern, large-scale, collaborative projects.

- Other systems like **Mercurial, Subversion**, and **Perforce** have their own strengths and are better suited for certain workflows or industries.

- **Choosing the right VCS** depends on your project's needs, team size, workflow preferences, and performance requirements.

- **Migrating to Git** from another VCS requires careful planning, training, and an understanding of both the challenges and benefits of Git.

In the next chapter, we will explore **advanced Git configurations** and tips for customizing Git to fit your team's specific workflow and requirements.

CHAPTER 26

GIT IN DEVOPS

Git has become a cornerstone in modern **DevOps** pipelines, which emphasize automation, collaboration, and continuous integration and deployment (CI/CD). It is no longer just a version control system for managing source code, but also plays an integral role in managing **infrastructure as code**, **automating testing**, and **deploying applications**. In this chapter, we will explore the **role of Git** in DevOps, how it integrates with **monitoring, testing**, and **deployment systems**, and provide a **real-world example** of managing infrastructure as code with Git.

The Role of Git in Modern DevOps Pipelines

DevOps pipelines are designed to enable the continuous integration, testing, and deployment of code, facilitating collaboration between development and operations teams. Git, as the most widely used version control system, plays a central role in these pipelines. Here's how Git fits into modern DevOps workflows:

1. **Source Control for Code and Configuration**:

   o In DevOps, Git is not just used for managing application code, but also for storing **infrastructure as code** (IaC) scripts, configuration files, and automation scripts. This ensures that both application and infrastructure changes are tracked in a single system.

   o Changes to code, infrastructure configurations, or automation scripts are all committed and pushed to the same Git repository, providing a single source of truth.

2. **Continuous Integration (CI)**:

   o Git acts as the source for triggering **CI** processes. When developers push code changes to a Git repository, it automatically triggers a build in the **CI system** (e.g., **Jenkins, GitHub Actions, Travis CI**). This process runs automated tests and checks to ensure that the code is functioning correctly before it is merged or deployed.

   o By integrating Git with CI systems, every commit can trigger tests and build processes, ensuring that errors are caught early in the development cycle.

3. **Continuous Delivery (CD)**:

   o **Continuous Delivery** involves automatically deploying code to production or staging environments after passing tests. Git's integration with **CD systems** (e.g., **GitLab CI**, **Azure DevOps, CircleCI**) ensures that once a commit is merged into a main or release branch, it automatically triggers a deployment pipeline.

   o The deployment process is often automated and tied to the Git workflow, ensuring that the correct version of the code is deployed without manual intervention.

4. **Versioning and Rollback**:

   o Git's ability to track the history of all code changes allows teams to easily **rollback** to previous versions in case of errors or failed deployments. This is particularly useful in production environments where changes need to be reversed quickly to maintain system stability.

o In DevOps, Git is integrated with deployment systems to roll back any deployments that fail, ensuring that any issues with new code are quickly rectified.

Integrating Git with Monitoring, Testing, and Deployment Systems

Git plays an essential role not only in code versioning but also in the integration and automation of monitoring, testing, and deployment systems. Here's how Git integrates with each part of the DevOps pipeline:

1. **Integrating Git with Monitoring Systems**:

   o **Monitoring systems** (e.g., **Prometheus, Grafana, New Relic**) track the health of applications and infrastructure, providing valuable insights into performance, resource usage, and potential bottlenecks.

   o Git can be used to **automatically deploy monitoring configurations** alongside code changes. For example, when you update your application's performance monitoring configurations or add new alerts, you commit those changes to Git. This allows operations teams to track the history of these configurations and apply them consistently across environments.

o Additionally, **GitOps** (a model where Git is used as the source of truth for both code and infrastructure) allows for automated updates of infrastructure monitoring based on changes committed to Git repositories.

2. **Integrating Git with Testing Systems**:

o **Automated testing** is a crucial part of the CI/CD pipeline, and Git seamlessly integrates with testing tools like **JUnit**, **Selenium**, and **Cypress**. When code is pushed to a Git repository, it triggers automated tests, ensuring that the new code does not break existing functionality.

o For example, if a developer pushes a commit to a Git branch, a **Jenkins** or **GitHub Actions** workflow can trigger:

- **Unit tests** to ensure the individual components work as expected.

307

- **Integration tests** to check if different modules interact correctly.

- **UI tests** to verify the user interface works as expected.

o Git can also be integrated with **code coverage tools** to monitor the extent of tests that are being run.

3. **Integrating Git with Deployment Systems:**

o **Git integration with deployment tools** (e.g., **Kubernetes, Docker, AWS, Azure DevOps**) ensures that code changes are automatically deployed to the appropriate environments.

o For example, you can configure a **GitHub Actions workflow** that:

- Triggers when a developer pushes code to the `main` branch.

- Runs automated tests.

- If the tests pass, deploys the code to a staging environment for further validation.

- Finally, if everything looks good in staging, it will automatically push the code to production.

This **automated deployment pipeline** reduces human error, improves efficiency, and accelerates the time it takes to get code from development to production.

Real-World Example: Managing Infrastructure as Code with Git

Scenario:

Your development team has been tasked with deploying and managing a **cloud infrastructure** for a web application. The team wants to implement **Infrastructure as Code (IaC)** and use **Git** as the source of truth for both application code and infrastructure configurations.

1. **Step 1: Set Up Infrastructure Code in Git**:
   - The team creates a Git repository to store all the infrastructure code. This includes configuration files for provisioning cloud resources (e.g., AWS EC2 instances, VPCs), load balancers, and security groups. Tools like **Terraform** or

309

CloudFormation are used to define the infrastructure in code.

o   Example structure:

```css
├── app/
│   └── src/
├── infrastructure/
│   ├── main.tf  # Terraform code for
infrastructure
│   └── outputs.tf  # Outputs from
Terraform
└── README.md
```

2.   **Step 2: Integrating Git with CI/CD Pipeline**:

o   The Git repository is integrated with a **CI/CD tool** like **Jenkins**, **GitHub Actions**, or **GitLab CI**. Each commit to the repository automatically triggers the following pipeline:

▪   **Testing**: The application code is built, and unit tests are executed.

▪   **Infrastructure Deployment**: If the commit includes updates to the infrastructure code, **Terraform** is used to apply changes to the cloud infrastructure.

```bash
terraform init
terraform apply -auto-approve
```

- **Deployment**: If the application tests pass, the application code is deployed to the cloud infrastructure.

3. **Step 3: Versioning Infrastructure with Git**:

   o Each change to the infrastructure (e.g., adding a new service, changing network configurations) is tracked in Git. Developers push changes to the infrastructure code, and Git history provides a full audit trail of what changes were made and when.

   o For example, if the team decides to update the server instance types in the cloud, they make the necessary changes to the `main.tf` file, commit the changes, and push them to the Git repository:

```bash
```

```
git commit -m "Update EC2 instance
type to t3.medium"
git push origin main
```

4. **Step 4: Rollback Using Git**:

   o If something goes wrong with the deployed infrastructure (e.g., new instances aren't provisioned correctly), the team can easily roll back by checking out a previous commit in Git and applying the infrastructure configurations again.

   bash

   ```
   git checkout <previous-commit-hash>
   terraform apply -auto-approve
   ```

5. **Step 5: Continuous Monitoring and Feedback Loop**:

   o After deployment, **monitoring tools** like **Prometheus** or **Grafana** continuously track the health of the infrastructure and the deployed application. Git and the CI/CD pipeline are integrated with the monitoring system to trigger automated actions (like scaling up infrastructure or redeploying the app) if performance issues are detected.

Key Takeaways:

- **Git's role in DevOps** is fundamental in modern workflows, integrating with CI/CD pipelines to automate testing, deployment, and infrastructure management.

- Git is not only used for managing application code but also for **infrastructure as code**, allowing teams to version and manage cloud resources.

- Git integrates with **monitoring systems**, **testing frameworks**, and **deployment tools**, forming the backbone of a fully automated, efficient DevOps pipeline.

- Using **GitOps** for managing infrastructure code through Git allows for seamless and consistent deployments, making it easier to manage complex environments and enabling faster iterations.

- Git's powerful branching and collaboration features, combined with CI/CD automation, ensure a smooth, efficient DevOps process, allowing for faster, more reliable software delivery.

In the next chapter, we will discuss **advanced Git configurations**, exploring how to fine-tune your Git setup to maximize performance and optimize collaboration in large teams.

CHAPTER 27

MASTERING GIT FOR COLLABORATIVE CODING

Git has become the cornerstone of modern software development, and mastering it can significantly enhance your ability to collaborate effectively with other developers, manage complex codebases, and streamline development workflows. Whether you're working alone or as part of a team, Git's powerful features can elevate your coding practices and ensure smooth, efficient collaboration. In this final chapter, we'll reflect on how to **become a Git master**, discuss the importance of **continuous learning**, and walk through a **real-world example** of how mastering Git can turn you into a key contributor to major software projects.

Final Thoughts on Becoming a Git Master

To truly master Git, you need to go beyond simply understanding basic commands. You must become proficient with Git's **advanced features**, **best practices**, and **strategies for collaboration.** Here are some final tips for mastering Git:

1. **Understand Git Internals:**

   o While you don't need to memorize every command or feature, having a deep understanding of how Git works **under the hood** can help you troubleshoot issues more effectively and use Git's advanced features with confidence.

   o Learn how Git stores data, how the staging area works, and how the commit history is managed. Understanding concepts like **branches**, **merges**, **rebases**, and **commits** will help you make more informed decisions while using Git.

2. **Master Branching and Merging:**

   o One of the core strengths of Git is its ability to handle branching and merging efficiently. Understanding when to use **feature branches**, **hotfix branches**, and **release branches** is essential.

   o Mastering merge strategies (like **fast-forward merges**, **three-way merges**, and **rebasing**) allows you to collaborate seamlessly with your team and avoid conflicts.

3. **Focus on Workflow Efficiency:**

- o Adopting efficient workflows like **Git Flow, GitHub Flow**, or **GitLab Flow** is key to managing collaborative projects effectively. Choose a workflow that suits your team size, project complexity, and release cycles.

- o Consistently applying Git best practices—such as **writing clear commit messages, frequent commits**, and **pull requests**—will ensure that your repository stays clean, understandable, and easy to navigate for other contributors.

4. **Collaborate and Contribute**:

- o To become a Git master, actively participate in open-source projects, contribute to team projects, and review other people's code. This will help you gain experience with **real-world Git workflows, branch management**, and **collaboration**.

- o Engage in **code reviews**, as reviewing others' code gives you a deeper understanding of best practices and teaches you how others handle challenges in version control.

Continuous Learning and Improvement with Git

Becoming a Git master is not a one-time achievement—it's a continuous learning process. As Git evolves and as you encounter new challenges, there's always more to learn. Here are some ways to continue your Git journey:

1. **Stay Updated with Git Releases**:
   - Git is an actively developed tool, and new features are regularly added. Stay updated with the latest releases and read the official **Git changelog** to learn about new features, improvements, and bug fixes.
   - GitHub and other platforms often provide tutorials and documentation for new features, so be sure to explore those resources to stay ahead.

2. **Experiment with Advanced Features**:
   - **Git bisect** for debugging, **Git stash** for saving unfinished work, **Git cherry-pick** for applying specific commits, and **Git submodules** for handling dependencies are just a few of the powerful features Git provides.

- o Experimenting with these features in personal or team projects will help you become more comfortable using them in real-world scenarios.

3. **Learn from Others**:

- o Follow blogs, podcasts, and community forums dedicated to Git and version control. Participate in online communities (e.g., **Stack Overflow, GitHub discussions**) to ask questions, share knowledge, and learn from others' experiences.

- o Explore **open-source projects** and study their Git workflows. Contributing to these projects is a great way to learn best practices from more experienced developers.

4. **Teach Git to Others**:

- o Teaching others is one of the best ways to solidify your own understanding of Git. Whether it's conducting training sessions for junior developers or writing blog posts about Git best practices, sharing knowledge helps reinforce your expertise.

Real-World Example: Becoming a Key Contributor to a Major Software Project Using Git

Scenario:

Imagine you're a developer working on a large-scale, collaborative **open-source software project**. The project is hosted on **GitHub**, and it has contributors from all over the world. The repository uses **Git Flow** as the workflow model, and contributions are organized via **feature branches** and **pull requests**.

1. **Step 1: Getting Started**:

   o As a new contributor, you first **fork the repository** and **clone it** to your local machine:

   ```bash
   git clone https://github.com/your-username/project-name.git
   ```

   o You review the **contributing guidelines** and set up your local development environment according to the instructions.

2. **Step 2: Creating a Feature Branch**:

o   You identify an issue in the project and decide to work on a fix. You start by creating a **feature branch** based on the develop branch:

bash

```
git checkout -b feature/fix-bug-123
develop
```

o   After making your changes and committing them with a clear, descriptive commit message:

bash

```
git commit -m "[BUG-123] Fix issue
with user authentication"
```

o   You push your feature branch to your forked repository:

bash

```
git push origin feature/fix-bug-123
```

3. **Step 3: Opening a Pull Request (PR):**

o   You open a **pull request** on **GitHub**, linking it to the related issue (e.g., **BUG-123**). The pull request includes a detailed explanation of what the change does and how it addresses the issue.

o Your PR is reviewed by the project maintainers and other contributors. They request some changes (e.g., better variable names or more test coverage).

4. **Step 4: Addressing Review Feedback:**

o You make the requested changes in your feature branch and update your pull request:

bash

```
git commit --amend
git push origin feature/fix-bug-123
--force
```

o The pull request is updated, and the maintainers verify that everything works as expected.

5. **Step 5: Merging Your PR:**

o After approval, your pull request is merged into the develop branch. The CI/CD pipeline runs automatically, triggering tests and deployments. Your contribution is now part of the main codebase.

322

6. **Step 6: Maintaining Contribution and Becoming a Core Contributor**:

   o As you continue to contribute to the project, you become more involved in discussions, code reviews, and decision-making. Your contributions increase in scope, and you eventually become a core contributor, responsible for reviewing pull requests, managing releases, and guiding the project's development.

   o You use **Git's advanced features** like **cherry-picking**, **bisecting**, and **rebasing** to handle complex merge issues and maintain a clean Git history for the project.

Key Takeaways:

- **Mastering Git** requires a deep understanding of branching, merging, and best practices. It also involves becoming comfortable with advanced features and workflows like **Git Flow** and **GitHub Flow**.

- **Continuous learning** is crucial to stay up-to-date with Git's evolving features and best practices. Experimenting with new Git features and engaging in the developer community can help you continuously improve your skills.

- **Real-world experience** with Git in collaborative projects, like contributing to open-source repositories, can elevate your Git expertise. Effective communication, code reviews, and following best practices will make you an invaluable contributor to any team or project.

- By consistently applying Git best practices, you'll not only improve your own workflow but also contribute to maintaining a clean, organized, and high-quality codebase for future developers.

In the next chapter, we will explore **advanced Git workflows** and discuss strategies for managing large teams and complex projects, helping you scale your Git practices for enterprise-level applications.